Accessing *the* Curriculum *for* Pupils *with* Autistic Spectrum Disorders

Using the TEACCH Programme to Help Inclusion

GARY MESIBOV AND MARIE HOWLEY

David Fulton Publishers

David Fulton Publishers
2 Park Square, Milton Park, Abingdon, Oxon OX14 4RN

270 Madison Avenue, New York, NY 10016

First published in Great Britain in 2003 by David Fulton Publishers
Transferred to digital printing

David Fulton Publishers is an imprint of the Taylor & Francis Group, an informa business

Copyright © 2003 Gary Mesibov and Marie Howley

British Library Cataloguing in Publication Data
A catalogue record for this book is available from the British Library.

ISBN 1-85346-795-2

Typeset by Kenneth Burnley, Wirral, Cheshire

Contents

Foreword

When I learnt of the collaboration that was to produce this book, I was very pleased. I am even more pleased to have the opportunity to write its foreword. Although I have long believed that no single approach has all the answers to working with individuals with Autistic Spectrum Disorders (ASD), I have been impressed with the TEACCH (Treatment and Education of Autistic and related Communication handicapped CHildren) approach in a number of ways. Prime among these is a statement Gary Mesibov made when I challenged him on the issue of 'single approaches' the first time I heard him speak. 'At TEACCH', he said, 'we have tried, and continue to try, to provide the best system we can for working with individuals with ASD. If others find better systems, then that is all to the good.'

That impressed me, because it seems to me that is all any of us can do. Unless we are only interested in selling a particular approach, we keep researching, keep listening to, and observing, individuals with ASD and the carers and professionals who work with them, and then try to provide services in the best way possible to meet all the needs we have identified and to help them develop their strengths and interests to ensure the best prospects for them in the future. They have a right to this as their entitlement to the 'broad and relevant' (I never can understand what 'balance' has to do with it) educational experience that the UK National Curriculum was meant to guarantee. They motivate those who work in the field to provide it because of their particular vulnerabilities.

The debate (although sometimes its undignified nature hardly merits the term) about particular interventions in ASD, often confuses two separate goals of education in ASD. The first is the goal of remediation, which is often predominant in early interventions. This views education as a kind of therapy, aiming to reduce or even eliminate the effects of autism on development. TEACCH has never made any extravagant claims about remediation and, indeed, tends to work *with* rather than *against* the autism. This can be seen both as more realistic and as more respectful of the individual's right to be different and the potential value of such difference. Naturally, that is not a message that many parents want to hear and for some individuals with ASD, the goal of remediation seems attractive against the misery and difficulties resulting from their autism. TEACCH does not see itself as obstructing or even delaying remediation but tends to the very educational view that we must start where the child is and help that child to develop and learn in the best way possible, for that individual, rather than against normative criteria.

The main strength of the TEACCH approach, however, is as a compensatory intervention. This is the one that fits best into the second main goal of education, that of entitlement to equality of opportunity in all aspects of life. That goal raises issues of access, and it is here that TEACCH has its main role – providing ways of enabling individuals with ASD to gain access to whatever educational opportunities are available to their peers in whatever setting. In much of the UK this will include the National Curriculum. This book provides very practical examples of how that can be accomplished. In the past, many teachers have associated specialist approaches with specialist settings. Yet it is in inclusive settings that they are most needed. Where the total environment cannot be fully geared to the child with an ASD, TEACCH provides principles and strategies for enabling effective differentiation of the curriculum to enable learning in pupils with ASD.

Any of the misunderstandings about TEACCH come from the way in which staff are often not fully trained and so associate TEACCH with paraphernalia rather than an approach based on individual assessment and tailored strategies, themselves based on research and observation of how children with ASD best learn. Once the principles underlying TEACCH have been grasped, it can be seen that it does not have to single out the child in a mainstream classroom, nor does it need to isolate the child in his/her learning in separate 'booths'. This book offers practical, yet principled, ways of managing an increasingly inclusive environment for children with ASD and their teachers, in whatever setting, without foregoing an intervention tailored to address their very particular needs. It is a timely addition to the growing stock of books on autism.

DR RITA JORDAN
Reader in Autism Studies
University of Birmingham
November 2002

Preface

This volume was inspired by the many parents and professionals in the UK who are using Division TEACCH's Structured Teaching and have asked us how it relates to the National Curriculum. After responding to many of these inquiries individually, we decided that it might be more efficient and helpful to organise our ideas and present them systematically. This is not a manual about Division TEACCH, nor how to implement Structured Teaching. Instead, it represents our effort to show how Division TEACCH's major intervention strategy, Structured Teaching, can be used to advance many of the goals and priorities that are enumerated in the National Curriculum.

Throughout this book we have used the term Autistic Spectrum Disorders (ASD) to describe our population of pupils who might find this most beneficial. This terminology corresponds to our view of autism as more than a single, finite developmental disability, but rather a continuum of difficulties, ranging from mild to severe, involving social problems, communication difficulties and narrow repetitive behaviours. We have taken the editorial prerogative of using the term 'he' to refer to our population. This was chosen because of the 4:1 ratio of males to females that is found throughout the autism literature.

This volume is the culmination of two years of hard work defining our main concepts, collecting information, generating figures, and then writing, rewriting and editing. We hope that these efforts will be of help to our many friends, colleagues, families and other interested citizens who have expressed an interest in this subject.

Acknowledgements

This book would not have been completed without the help of many dedicated people. Firstly we are grateful to the contributors who gave up their valuable time, and sometimes their classrooms, to provide examples and illustrations of their professional practice. This has ensured that the examples provided are 'real'.

Thanks go to Eileen Arnold, Terence Arnold, David Preece and Richard Rose for their conscientious reading, feedback and suggestions. Their inspiration has been invaluable. Thanks also to the Centre for Special Needs Education and Research (CeSNER) team at University College Northampton who provided continual support and encouragement, and to Joan Berry for her efficient, and always cheerful, assistance with typing.

Finally a special thank you to the children and their families who make sure that we know when the structure is working.

Contributors

Green Oaks Lower School, Designated Special Provision (DSP): Northamptonshire
Kingsley Special School: Northamptonshire
Kingsthorpe Grove Lower School, DSP: Northamptonshire
Linden Bridge School: Surrey
Peak School: Derbyshire
Radlett Lodge, The National Autistic Society: Hertfordshire
Rowan Gate Primary School: Northamptonshire
Samuel Whitbread Community College: Bedfordshire
Special Educational Needs and Psychology Service: Essex
Sunfield School: Worcestershire

Permissions

The Picture Communication System© 1981–2002, Mayer-Johnson, Inc. Used with permission. Mayer-Johnson, Inc., PO Box 1579, Solana Beach, CA 92075, USA
Tel.: 858 550 0084; Fax: 858 550 0449
Web site: www.mayer-johnson.com
Email: mayerj@mayer-johnson.com

Widgit Rebus Symbols used with permission from Widgit Software Ltd.
Widgit Software Ltd, 124 Cambridge Science Park, Milton Road, Cambridge, CB4 0ZS.

Dedicated to Terry Arnold who did so much to improve the lives of people with autism in the world and especially in playing a pivotal role in bringing the TEACCH ideas to the UK.

1 Overview of the autistic spectrum

Autistic Spectrum Disorders

The word 'autism' first appeared in the professional literature when Leo Kanner, a child psychiatrist at Johns Hopkins University in Baltimore, MD, wrote a description of 11 children from his child psychiatric unit in 1943. These children were different from the others in his unit who were diagnosed with Childhood Schizophrenia. The children Kanner wrote about in his original paper had little interest in other people, peculiar language, an insistence on routines, and they displayed unusual body movements and repetitive behaviours.

Kanner's original description emphasised three areas of difficulty: social isolation, abnormal communication and an insistence on repetitive, narrow routines. These major areas of impairment have continued to be the foundation of the autism diagnosis in the major diagnostic systems used throughout the world.

Although this 'triad of impairments' (Wing and Gould 1979) has always been central to the diagnosis of autism, it has also been acknowledged that it is possible to have more subtle deficits or peculiarities in these three areas without having the full autism syndrome. For this reason, the term Pervasive Developmental Disorders (PDD) was created as the umbrella category of all people showing impairments or peculiarities in these three areas, including more subtle ones. More recently, the term Autistic Spectrum Disorders (ASD) is replacing PDD as the umbrella term for the triad of impairments. This term is preferred by most professionals who believe that autism is the central and most widely known disability among this group and for this reason this term (autism) should be part of any phrase describing the broader syndrome.

Current diagnostic systems, DSM-IV (American Psychiatric Association 1994) and ICD-10 (WHO 1992), usually define autism based on a series of specific social, communication and restricted behaviours. In order to qualify for the autism diagnosis, a person must demonstrate deficits in each of these three areas and the requirement is that the social deficit or peculiarity will be especially marked. Many individuals with ASD will also have additional learning difficulties.

Although autism is the best-known and most widely used diagnostic category within the autistic spectrum, there are several other specific diagnostic classifications as well. These other classifications are distinguishable from classical autism because of their characteristics, but most of the needs of this group and the intervention techniques that have proven effective are similar to those used for children and adults classified with the autism diagnosis.

Pervasive Developmental Disorders. Not Otherwise Specified (PDD.NOS), sometimes referred to as Atypical Autism, refers to those people on the autistic spectrum who share many of the characteristics but don't meet the criteria for classical autism. These people might not show the precise number of characteristics required for the autism diagnosis or they might not have the marked deficits or peculiarities in the social area that are necessary. PDD.NOS also does not require the full triad of impairments; people classified with this diagnosis can have impairments in either communication or restricted behaviours, but not necessarily both. Many professionals view PDD.NOS (Atypical Autism) as a milder form of autism.

Another diagnosis that falls within the autistic spectrum is Asperger Syndrome (AS). This category was named after an Austrian paediatrician, Hans Asperger, who began his work at about the same time as Kanner in the early 1940s. Unlike Kanner, who lived in the USA and wrote in English, Asperger's paper was written in German and published during the middle of World War II. For these reasons, it was not widely read by the American and British professionals, who have been the most influential investigators in the field since its inception. In 1981 Lorna Wing, an eminent British psychiatrist and a parent of a child with autism, translated the paper into English and it has had a major impact ever since.

The definition of AS is similar to autism. In fact, the social and restricted interest characteristics are identical. The difference is in the area of communication; a person does not have to demonstrate any communication difficulties to qualify for the AS diagnosis. In fact, it is a requirement that their language develops at the normal time, using words by the age of two and simple phrases by age three. For a diagnosis of AS, it is also required that a person have an average or above average IQ. A dual diagnosis of autism and AS is impossible under the present systems; if a person qualifies for the diagnosis of autism, then the additional diagnosis of AS is not permitted. AS is, therefore, an ASD, including higher intellectually functioning clients with excellent language skills. They generally have more self-awareness than others on the autistic spectrum and also more subtle social deficits.

Two other less common diagnoses have been identified as part of the autistic spectrum. Both of these involve severe deterioration after a period of normal development. These diagnoses are Rett's Disorder and Childhood Disintegrative Disorder. Rett's Disorder, found only in girls, usually appears after a period of normal development for up to six months and sometimes even longer. The disorder starts with a loss of interest and skills in social interaction, a deceleration in head circumference growth and brain development, and a loss of speech, thinking and motor skills. One of the most severe aspects of the motor impairments is the loss of hand use. Purposeful hand manipulations are replaced by repetitive wringing, clapping, or rubbing of hands in the middle of the body. Girls with Rett's Disorder usually have severe learning difficulties.

Childhood Disintegrative Disorder is similar to Rett's Disorder, because it involves a period of normal development followed by a loss of skills, resulting in severe cognitive, social and motor impairments. Childhood Disintegrative Disorder is different, however, because it affects both boys and girls and, in fact, is much more common in boys. The period of normal development is much longer than with Rett's Disorder; the regression does not occur until right after the age of two and sometimes later than that. Childhood

Disintegrative Disorder does not include the repetitive hand movements that are so typical of Rett's Disorder and that so dominate their activities.

To summarise, the ASDs include a series of conditions characterised by social, communication and restrictive behavioural difficulties. Autism is the most common and widely known of these disabilities. PDD.NOS is a milder form of ASD, which includes impairments in each, or at least most, of these areas but in a milder form or to a less substantial degree. AS includes those people who do not meet the full criteria for autism because of less impaired communication skills, and who are functioning intellectually in the normal to above normal range. Rett's Disorder and Childhood Disintegrative Disorder appear after periods of normal development and involve severe impairments in cognitive, communication and motor functioning.

Overlapping disorders

It is a major challenge identifying people with ASDs and determining where they appear on the continuum. It is also difficult to distinguish ASDs from related conditions because there are sometimes significant areas of overlap. Diagnoses with the greatest overlap that are most frequently confused with ASDs are Obsessive-Compulsive Disorder (OCD), Semantic-Pragmatic Disorder, Attention Deficit Hyperactivity Disorder (ADHD) and Schizoid Personality Disorder.

Obsessive-Compulsive Disorder is identified by repetitive thoughts and/or behaviours. A distinction is usually made between obsessions, which are recurrent and persistent thoughts, and compulsions, which are non-functional repetitive behaviours. Sometimes the distinctions between OCD and ASDs are difficult to distinguish because many people with ASDs have repetitive thoughts or behaviours. Some differences that help professionals make these discriminations are that most people with OCD are secretive about their repetitive ideas or behaviours because they realise that other people would consider them bizarre. Those affected with OCD usually wish that the routines would go away and feel great anxiety when thinking about or performing them. This is very different from people with ASDs, who have little insight into the non-productive nature of their repetitive behaviours or how these behaviours impact on others. Often people with ASDs feel calm and relaxed when thinking about and performing their rituals, rather than anxious.

It is important for clinicians to understand that the narrow interests associated with ASDs are not the same as obsessive thoughts. The preoccupations that these youngsters think and talk about are much less likely to be the sex, religion, or bodily concerns that are more frequently seen in OCD. Developmental histories can also be helpful in making these distinctions. People with OCD usually do not have preschool or early onset of these preoccupations and other developmental difficulties. The earlier onset of these obsessions or compulsions, plus other developmental problems, are much more typical in ASDs.

Semantic-Pragmatic Disorder (Bishop 2000) is a developmental language disorder characterised by problems in language content and comprehension (semantics) and function (pragmatics). These difficulties occur in spite of near-normal grammar, vocabulary and speech production. People who fall within this diagnostic classification show several similarities to ASDs. They have problems with some of the same aspects of interpersonal communication, including difficulties initiating and sustaining conversations, staying on topics, using words appropriately in context, and understanding subtleties. These difficulties are so substantial and so similar that some investigators question whether Semantic-Pragmatic Disorder should be a separate diagnosis from the autistic spectrum (Gagnon *et al.* 1997). In their study, Gagnon and his colleagues found that an overwhelming majority of children diagnosed with Semantic-Pragmatic Disorder in the UK also fitted a diagnosis for the autistic spectrum and very few of these children did not. Therefore, they argue that it does not seem reasonable to have a separate diagnostic category for so few children.

In spite of the controversy, there are some differences between Semantic-Pragmatic Disorders and ASDs. Szatmari (1998) found that children with Semantic-Pragmatic Disorder usually have delayed milestones, which differentiate them from children with ASD. It has been noted, however, that there are certain problems with this aspect of the ASD definition so this distinction might not be relevant when the diagnostic category is revised. Children with Semantic-Pragmatic Disorders are also unlikely to have social interaction problems beyond those already mentioned in social communication. They also do not demonstrate other communication difficulties, problems with imaginative play, or narrow, restricted interests.

Although the diagnostic category of Semantic-Pragmatic Disorder is popular in many places, especially the UK, it has not yet been incorporated in any of the major diagnostic classification systems and there is some question of whether it represents a meaningful entity that is separate from the ASDs. This category will be interesting to watch as the current diagnostic systems evolve.

Another diagnostic category that overlaps with ASD is Attention Deficit Hyperactivity Disorder (ADHD). ADHD is used to describe people who have difficulty paying attention and controlling their behaviour and activity levels. People in this group can often resemble people with ASD because they appear not to listen when addressed, they have difficulty following verbal directions, problems with concentration, a reluctance to engage in certain tasks, problems with impulse control, and excessive talking.

Even though there are many similarities between ADHD and ASD, the underlying reasons for the difficulties are usually different. For children with ADHD, there appears to be a neurological problem limiting their focused attention that can have implications for social and communication difficulties. It is not that these children can't understand language or social nuances, it is rather that they have difficulty focusing their attention in appropriate ways at appropriate times. For people with autism, their problem is not necessarily limited attention but rather a different way of focusing their attention. It has been suggested that their focus is more narrow and intense and that they also have difficulty shifting their attention. Social and communication difficulties for people with autism are usually the reasons why they have problems communicating and also with understanding and responding to directions. It is these social and communication problems that make interaction difficult, in addition to their attentional differences, rather than simply their attentional problems.

A final condition that is sometimes confused with ASD is Schizoid Personality Disorder. This disorder is characterised by a 'pervasive pattern of detachment from social relationships and a restricted range of expression of emotions in interpersonal settings' (DSM-IV American Psychiatric Association 1994: 638). Problems with social skills and friendship, aloofness, an apparent insensitivity to others and a narrow single-mindedness are characteristics that this group shares with people with ASD. The differences, however, are that people with Schizoid Personality Disorder have less severe problems with interpersonal relationships and they manifest themselves later in the school years or in early adulthood, rather than in the preschool and early school years, as is seen with ASD. Communication problems among the Schizoid Personality Group are also more limited. This group shows a capacity for imagination and fantasy and they do not have the narrow special interests of people with ASD. There also seems to be a genetic link between Schizoid Personality Disorder and other psychiatric conditions.

In spite of these differences, Wolff (1998) argues that Schizoid Personality Disorder might be part of the autistic spectrum. She argues that many of the effective intervention approaches used with higher functioning people with ASD can also be used effectively with this group, even though they are slightly more socially skilled, independent, and have a better long-term prognosis.

Summary

In summary, those who receive a diagnosis of ASD have many important similarities to one another, especially in the areas of social interaction, communication, perserveration and conceptualisation. These common characteristics have important implications for educational programmes and provision and will be the major focus of this book. Pupils with overlapping, but different, diagnoses will share enough common characteristics that they will probably benefit from some of the educational strategies described in the chapters that follow.

2 Structured Teaching as a foundation for educational programmes

Division TEACCH

Division TEACCH (Treatment and Education of Autistic and related Communication handicapped CHildren) is North Carolina's statewide programme serving people with ASD and their families. The programme was initially funded by the Federal Government in 1966. At that point, autism was viewed as an emotional disorder and parents were seen as the main cause. Terms like 'refrigerator mother' were commonly used to describe these parents and convey how cold, aloof and sometimes rejecting behaviours might cause autism in their children.

Eric Schopler, co-founder and the first Director of Division TEACCH, was among the pioneers in establishing autism as a developmental disorder and demonstrating that parents did not cause autism and could be effective teachers of their children. This was the focus of the initial Federal grant to Schopler that was the precursor to Division TEACCH in 1966. The Federal grant was enormously successful and had an immediate positive impact on the parents who participated and their children. For this reason, the state of North Carolina adopted Division TEACCH statewide and initiated state funding in its founding legislation in 1972.

Over the past three decades, Division TEACCH has helped to reconceptualise theories about autism and has created a successful and widely used intervention approach. TEACCH has also implemented a comprehensive service delivery system that has impacted on the lives of over 5,000 people with autism and their families in North Carolina and many others throughout the world. The programme's major priorities include:

- enabling individuals with ASD to function meaningfully, productively and as independently as possible in their communities;
- to offer exemplary services to individuals with ASD and their families and those who work with them and support them; and
- as a member of the University of North Carolina community, to generate knowledge, to integrate theory with clinical practice and to disseminate information about theory and practice internationally.

Division TEACCH has a zero reject policy and therefore serves people with ASD of all ages and levels of functioning. Starting with diagnostic evaluations that typically occur between the ages of two and four, families first learn about the disability of autism from TEACCH staff, who work out of nine clinical centres geographically distributed throughout the state of North Carolina. Each clinic serves families of people with ASD from ages 1 to 70 years in their local regions. About 80 per cent of the initial visits are for children under the age of five.

Division TEACCH integrates a community-based service system into a vibrant University, which encourages the accomplishment of programme goals at a high level of excellence. TEACCH offers the best of what universities are capable of for the benefit of the citizens of the state of North Carolina, including unique opportunities for training, service development, and research. The base at the University of North Carolina also allows families easy access to the latest developments in the field and is a wonderful resource for recruiting qualified professionals who often become leaders in the field.

The active involvement of the TEACCH programme in community-based activities also adds to the University's lustre and credibility. By requiring a University faculty to be actively involved in solving day-to-day needs, there is assurance that the programme will not become an ivory tower. Confronting the compelling needs of families and clients with ASD assures that the University-based programme will be working on important and relevant issues.

As part of the state system, Division TEACCH is well positioned to coordinate and collaborate with a variety of state agencies. Transitions from early intervention to school programmes are smoother because TEACCH is available to work closely with each agency and the families. A consistent intervention strategy also facilitates transitions from one programme to the next. Division TEACCH tries to maintain strong collaborative relationships with major state agencies and also the parent advocacy group, the Autism Society of North Carolina.

Although the statewide system is an important reason for TEACCH's many accomplishments, the programme is not just a coordinating and facilitating agency. Through the programme's experiences over the past 30 years and with the help of its University base, Division TEACCH has evolved its own treatment strategy and approach to working with clients with ASD and their families. This approach, called Structured Teaching, assures continuity and consistency throughout all of the statewide services for people with ASD and their families.

The strategies and administrative structures from Division TEACCH have been implemented throughout the USA and all over the world. Practitioners and administrators have been using these ideas in each of the 50 states in America. Many states have set up TEACCH Structured Teaching educational programmes and there are also numerous clinics and other services following these models. Internationally, these techniques are practised throughout Europe, Asia and South America. These approaches have also had a major impact in the UK.

TEACCH in the UK

TEACCH strategies were first introduced into the UK on a large scale around 1990, as a result of recommendations made by an interagency working party. Regular TEACCH seminars, sponsored by the Society for the Autistically Handicapped

(SFTAH), now Autism Independent UK, began in Kettering, in collaboration with the local authority. Other local authorities (e.g. Bedfordshire) and special schools (e.g. Sunfield) followed soon afterwards and consequently Autism Independent UK, Bedfordshire and Sunfield have organised training activities regularly in collaboration with Division TEACCH. The National Autistic Society has also collaborated with Division TEACCH on regular training programmes throughout the UK since the mid-1990s. In the decade starting with the early 1990s, close to 15,000 parents and professionals have been trained in the Structured Teaching strategies through collaborative training programmes between Division TEACCH and local British parent, professional and school organisations. These training programmes continue around the country on a regular basis throughout the year and many teachers now make use of Structured Teaching for pupils with ASD.

Structured Teaching

The concept of Structured Teaching grew out of Division TEACCH's early recognition of autism as a developmental disorder. When TEACCH was established in the mid-1960s, most professionals viewed autism as an emotional disorder, caused by parent ambivalence, rejection and inconsistent responses to their children. Eric Schopler, the co-founder of Division TEACCH, was one of the pioneers to recognise autism as a developmental disorder involving neurological differences from the ways in which typically developing children processed the environment. Structured Teaching evolved as a way of matching educational practices to the different ways that people with ASD understand, think and learn. Structured Teaching is designed to address the major neurological differences in autism.

Receptive language difficulties are other important characteristics of ASD that Structured Teaching addresses. Many pupils with ASD cannot understand language as well as we think they can, based on their other skills and responses. They also have difficulty initiating responses to our verbal requests. Receptive language difficulties can result in a limited understanding of what appear to be relatively simple requests.

Expressive communication can also be difficult. Language often falls behind other skills for people with autism so their responses or ability to express simple requests can be limited. Expressive communication requires a degree of initiation, organisation and comprehension that is sometimes beyond what these otherwise skilled youngsters with autism can produce. This often results in frustration on everyone's part because they cannot express many of their needs in ways that allow others to meet those needs.

Attention and memory can also be different in people with ASD. Although their ability to recall specific details over long periods of time is legendary, working memory, or the ability to process several pieces of information at the same time, is often impaired. People with ASD can have problems attending to the most relevant aspects of situations or to verbal statements that are presented to them. Organisation is another major concern, both organising materials and activities, in both space and time. Familiar material is processed more readily than novelty and there appears to be a strong preference for comfortable activities and routines that have been repeated before.

Other challenges for people with ASD are dealing with other people and also sensory stimulation in the environment. People with ASD do not have an intuitive grasp of others' motivations and behaviours. Social rules are mysterious to them. These can result in inappropriate behaviours designed to gain the attention of other people, social withdrawal, or a preference for being alone. The lack of social relatedness can also make initiatives from other people ineffective in motivating and directing behaviour.

Sensory stimulation can be especially distracting. People with ASD can overreact to stimulation in the environment and have difficulty modulating its impact. Behaviour problems frequently result from their inability to deal with sensory input.

Structured Teaching is a system of organising the classroom and making teaching processes and styles autism-friendly. Expectations are made concrete and clear to people with ASD. It is a system of structuring educational programmes taking into account skills, deficits and interests of people with ASD. Emphasis is placed on understanding and meeting individual needs, rather than judging student appropriateness or compatibility with some implicit or explicit model of social and cognitive 'normalcy'. For example, many people with ASD have much stronger visual skills compared with auditory skills. Structured Teaching allows them to utilise these strengths by presenting information and instructions visually. Visual information makes things more meaningful for people with ASD and enables them to function more independently and to learn. The main purpose of Structured Teaching is to increase independence and to manage behaviour by considering the cognitive skills, needs and interests of people with ASD and adjusting the environment accordingly. If we are successful in this, the use of Structured Teaching can also facilitate both teaching and learning. There are four components of Structured Teaching that are incorporated into any educational programme: physical structure, daily schedules, work systems, and visual structure and information.

Physical structure

Physical structure and organisation makes the classroom interesting, clear and manageable for pupils with ASD. The physical layout of the classroom is an important first step in assuring that a programme will be conducive to the learning styles, needs and sensory peculiarities of pupils with ASD. Individual needs must be considered when planning the physical arrangement of the classroom. Where and how the furniture is placed can affect each pupil's ability to deal with the environment, understand its expectations and function independently. Clear visual information can reduce anxiety and promote independence. The physical structure of the classroom can also minimise distractions, promoting more consistent and effective work.

Every pupil in every classroom will not require the same degree of structure. For pupils with ASD who need self-contained classrooms, developing specific areas for specific learning activities, marking clear boundaries, and assuring that materials are easily accessible helps them to know where they are supposed to go and allows them to secure their materials independently. More able pupils in mainstream classrooms may not need the same degree of physical structure to direct their activities. For these pupils, areas in the regular classroom where there is not as much activity are good to locate and establish as places for them to work. It is usually helpful for them to have a quiet place where they can go from time to time when the noise, visual images and smells of the regular classroom become overbearing.

Ages of the pupils will also impact on the physical structure. A classroom with younger pupils will need areas for play, independent and individual work, snack, the development of self-help skills, and possibly a bathroom for toilet training. Older pupils would need places to pursue their leisure interests, areas for vocational skills, and places for domestic and self-help skills, along with the parts of the classroom needed for independent and one-to-one academic studies, group work and whole-class teaching.

No matter what the level of ability, materials should be clearly marked and arranged at each student's level of understanding. Work materials should obviously be available in pupils' academic areas, while play or leisure materials should be available at the time and place where these are appropriate. Easy access to materials at the time when they are likely to be used is important for pupils at every age and level of functioning.

For all pupils with ASD there are some particularly important considerations in establishing their work areas. This is because of the importance of these areas for developing appropriate independent academic and vocational skills and the difficulty pupils with ASD often have in blocking out distractions so that they can focus on the most relevant and important aspects of their tasks. Work areas have to provide opportunities for independent and group work. For pupils with ASD who are easily distracted, work areas should be located in the least stimulating sections of the classroom, away from other pupils in places with minimal distractions. Some pupils with ASD might be able to work next to their peers, but even they may benefit from working consistently in the same place on each of their assignments each day. There should be clearly marked areas to place finished work, even for the most able pupils. Easily accessible and clearly marked work materials should be readily available. Additional areas in these classrooms should be established for group work, whole-class teaching, leisure, play, or just relaxation, depending on the needs of the pupils.

Often overlooked, the physical structure of the classroom can be an extremely important variable in the success or failure of a pupil with ASD. Carefully considering the pupil's conceptual and sensory needs can result in a classroom environment that promotes learning and independent functioning.

Schedules

Pupils with ASD require predictability and clarity. To the extent that we can meet those needs, we are generally rewarded with calmer and more cooperative behaviour because the pupils understand exactly what they are supposed to do. The TEACCH programme incorporates individualised daily schedules as a way of meeting those compelling needs. These schedules, if organised meaningfully with an understanding of each pupil's individual skills, can add order, predictability and organisation to their lives.

It has already been discussed how frequently pupils with ASD have difficulties with sequential memory and organisation. Receptive language difficulties can also make it hard for pupils to understand what is expected, which often leads to their resisting part of the curriculum. Schedules not only direct specific activities as they are occurring, but they also reduce anxiety by helping pupils organise, understand and anticipate their daily activities.

In addition to adding predictability and clarity to their lives, daily schedules offer the opportunity for pupils with ASD to move around their classrooms and schools independently of adult prompting and direction. This is very important for their feelings of autonomy and also helps them to become less prompt-dependent. Pupils who can follow their schedules independently are not as frequently overstimulated as pupils who are constantly prompted and cued and generally confused about where they are going and what is happening.

Checking their schedules regularly can also facilitate transitions, which can be difficult for them. Schedules provide a comfortable, predictable and consistent routine for pupils when they are navigating from one activity to the next. They offer a structure, foundation and comfortable routine that helps make the difficult process of changing from activity to activity easier and less anxiety-provoking.

The most typical formats for daily schedules, and the one that most of us use, are written in the form of timetables and diaries. Our own schedules typically include the entire day. Unfortunately, many pupils with ASD have difficulty understanding the written word and cannot conceptualise a full day at a time. For these pupils, the schedule can consist of pictures or drawings, representing their activities. For example, a picture of a desk or table can represent their work time; a picture of a swing can represent outdoor playtime. It is also possible to use objects, if these are what the pupil most readily understands. Toilet paper for a pupil using this system might indicate the toilet, a backpack might indicate it is time to go home, or a floppy disk might be the indication that it is time to use the computer. For pupils whose organisational difficulties make a full day hard to conceptualise, their schedules can be presented to them one-half day at a time, three activities at a time, or even one activity at a time. The important thing is that the type of schedule and the number of items presented are at the pupil's level of understanding.

Work system

The daily schedule is important to indicate the sequence of events during the pupil's day. It is a critical factor in keeping pupils focused and enabling them to understand what will be happening to them. The schedule is one way of organising pupils with ASD in the classroom. Another is the work system, which helps them to organise each specific activity that they are involved with. Work systems are critical if pupils with ASD are to learn to work without adult assistance or direct supervision. They help pupils to know what is expected of them on each of their specific work activities so that they can organise themselves systematically and complete their tasks independent of adult assistance where appropriate. Work systems can also be used to facilitate paired and group learning activities.

Individual work systems communicate four pieces of information to the pupils:

1. What work they are supposed to do.
2. How much work (or how many tasks) will be required at this specific time.
3. How they know they are making progress and when they have finished.
4. What happens after the work is completed.

11

As with effective schedules, work systems are presented visually on a level that each individual can understand and practised regularly until they can be used independently in a variety of settings.

Work systems, like schedules, differ based on the pupils who are using them. A written work system might be useful for a pupil who can read and understand written language easily, with each task clearly labelled, making it easy to locate. The pupil would know what to do by what was written on the work system corresponding to the labels on his work. He would know how much work by the number of items written on the work system for that particular time period. He would also know that the task was completed when each of the written directions was carried out and crossed off. There would also be a written explanation of what would happen after the task was completed.

Written work systems are used for pupils who can read and understand language easily; pictures, symbols, numbers, colours or objects can communicate the same information for pupils who do not read. A pupil at this level might have a work system consisting of different colours arranged as a top to bottom list. Each colour would correspond to a colour label on a visually clear task. The pupil would know what task to do by matching the colour on the work system to the work labelled with the same colour. He would know 'how much' by the number of coloured circles from top to bottom. If there were three circles, that would mean that there were three tasks to complete during the work session. The pupil would also know that the work was completed when all three of the circles had been removed from the work system. Progress would be understood by seeing each of the circles disappear after each specific task was completed. The consequence for the pupil after successfully completing the task could be a picture at the bottom of the work system, indicating what he can do next. The picture could indicate a computer activity or the art area and the child would know to go there after completing the work session.

Work systems help to organise specific work activities. They provide meaningful, organised and effective ways of carrying out specific tasks. They also make the concept of 'finished' concrete and meaningful for individual pupils. Understanding this concept gives the pupils a feeling of completion and makes moving from one activity to another, traditionally difficult for pupils with autism, a more meaningful process and therefore less anxiety provoking. Knowing how much work one has to complete and having a sense of making progress toward the completion can be of great assistance to pupils with ASD.

Visual structure and information

Up to this point, we have described the organisational systems for moving from place to place (schedule) and for completing specific activities in a variety of different places (work systems). Structured Teaching is also important when thinking about and creating the activities or academic tasks themselves. Each task should be visually organised and structured to minimise anxiety by maximising clarity, understanding and interests. Three components of the activities are especially crucial for achieving these positive results: visual clarity, visual organisation and visual instructions.

Visual clarity

One way of providing visual structure is through clarification. Clarifying important components of a task and essential expectations for pupils with ASD can greatly improve their ability to successfully complete these tasks with minimal anxiety. A sorting task can have visually clear shapes or colours and that might help them highlight the essential dimension on which sorting will occur. A carpeted section of the classroom with bright squares might remind the pupils that this is the place for their leisure activities. Highlighting relevant and important aspects of worksheets can also be helpful, e.g. highlighting which sentence in each paragraph has the most relevant information or which letter of a word is crucial for alphabetising.

Visual organisation

Visual organisation involves the distribution and stability of the materials that pupils use in completing their tasks. Pupils with ASD are frequently distracted and disrupted if their materials are not neatly organised and stable. They can easily be overwhelmed, or at least distracted, by sensory disorganisation. Pupils with ASD seem to lack the ability to organise their materials themselves so it is essential for teachers and other professionals to order their materials in an attractive, orderly and minimally stimulating fashion. For example, on a sorting task involving a variety of materials, pupils with ASD are usually more successful and less anxious if the materials are neatly distributed in cups, rather than spread out loosely on the table in front of them in a big pile.

In addition to neatly organising materials, it is also helpful if large spaces are broken down into smaller components. Pupils with ASD have difficulty organising themselves and larger surfaces can compound this problem. A pupil washing a large table will probably do better if it is divided into four smaller squares, rather than having to take on the entire surface at one time. A complex worksheet may be organised into clear sections to help a pupil complete it.

Visual instructions

Visual instructions are the final type of visual structure. Visual instructions are essential components of work tasks. They provide visual information to pupils with ASD that explain on their level of understanding exactly what is required for task completion. A common form of visual instruction is a jig, or visual representation, of how materials are to be placed, or how a task is to be carried out. Written instructions can also serve this function, explaining to the student exactly what is expected or required.

Visual instructions are essential components of Structured Teaching tasks for several reasons. First, they help pupils to understand exactly what they are supposed to do, a certainty that is essential for most pupils with ASD. Visual instructions also allow for a degree of flexibility that is often not seen in ASD. If a pupil with ASD learns to complete a task in a specific way, it is usually extremely difficult to alter his strategy or approach to the materials. Through visual instructions, however, we have a mechanism for changing their approach when necessary. Because the pupil is responding to the instructions, changing those instructions can alter the responses and result in a pupil following a different procedure with the same set of materials. This allows a degree of flexibility that is uncommon in ASD, but essential for effective learning and vocational and community functioning.

Conclusion

In conclusion, the TEACCH programme, now completing its fourth decade as the statewide programme for people with ASD in North Carolina, continues to refine the concept that people with ASD function differently from people without ASD in terms of their thinking and learning and have specialised learning needs, based on these differences. Structured Teaching has evolved as a teaching strategy responsive to these individualised needs that characterise people with ASD. Physically structuring environments, using schedules and work systems, and developing visually clear and organised materials, are the central components of this approach. Pupils with ASD who use this approach are calmer, more self-assured and are able to work productively and independently for longer periods of time. The use of Structured Teaching, as a method of delivering the curriculum, can enhance and facilitate the teaching and learning process and can improve access to the curriculum for many pupils with ASD.

3 The National Curriculum: challenges to access for pupils with Autistic Spectrum Disorders

Introduction

Pupils with ASD have specific learning needs and styles that must be addressed if they are to access the curriculum (organisation of the curriculum is outlined in Appendix A) in a meaningful way. The characteristics of ASD, arising from the triad of impairments (Wing and Gould 1979) and associated features, frequently mean that pupils may not understand or interpret the curriculum in the same way as other pupils. Challenges in the areas of communication, social interaction and imagination, together with a consideration of the thinking and learning styles of pupils with ASD must lead to a consideration of *how* the curriculum is best taught. Traditional teaching styles and curriculum delivery rely on social and verbal communication between adults and children. Meaning in the classroom is derived from a shared understanding of the social context in which all participants need to understand the classroom 'culture'. Powell (2000) emphasises the importance of 'meaning' for pupils with ASD. He suggests that 'meaning is central to our socially constructed way of living', the link between learning and meaning depending upon our cultural and social way of life. Pupils with ASD often do not understand the meaning, explicit or implicit, within the social classroom context. Sainsbury suggests that pupils with Asperger Syndrome are frequently 'oblivious' to the social context of the classroom and recalls her own experience when she felt as if 'everybody is playing some complicated game and I am the only one who hasn't been told the rules' (Sainsbury 2000: 8). This clearly has implications for teaching and learning as the unique characteristics and learning styles of pupils with ASD mean that they think in different ways to those who do not have ASD. A 'culture of autism' may be a helpful perspective in reminding us of the need to respect and accommodate their individual differences (Mesibov and Shea undated). Consequently, the culture of the classroom needs therefore to reflect their different 'culture' and thinking styles in order to increase their understanding.

Traditional teaching approaches, relying upon understanding social and verbal communication, may not be in the best interests of pupils with ASD, who are often unintentionally excluded from accessing the curriculum due to their different learning styles. The individual learning styles of those pupils with ASD must be taken into account when considering both the content and the delivery of the whole curriculum. Schools and communities that embrace the principles of 'entitlement' and 'inclusion' need to have a clear understanding of the individual learning needs of pupils with ASD, which takes into account cognitive learning styles and areas of strength.

This book is concerned with facilitating meaningful access to all aspects of the curriculum through the use of Structured Teaching, as advocated by Division TEACCH (Schopler *et al.* 1995). It is acknowledged that one single approach is unlikely to be successful for every pupil with ASD, given the range of ability and individual differences across the spectrum (Jordan *et al.* 1998). Visual structure is nevertheless increasingly recognised as one potentially useful approach both in specialist and in mainstream classrooms (e.g. Cumine *et al.* 1998, DfES 2001a, 2002, Hodgdon 1995, Quill 1995).

Structured Teaching is particularly helpful when considering how best to deliver the curriculum to facilitate access in a meaningful way. The approach takes into account our understanding of the cognitive processes of pupils with ASD and in particular focuses on areas of strength in visual cognition. In addition Structured Teaching is flexible, taking into account individual learning needs and the differing demands of the class-room contexts in which pupils with ASD are found. The particular challenges to access and entitlement for pupils with ASD are the focus of this discussion, with an emphasis on implications for curriculum delivery. Subsequent chapters provide detailed illustrative examples of how teachers in the UK are applying the principles of Structured Teaching to enable pupils to access the whole curriculum.

Entitlement for pupils with ASD

Since its introduction in 1989, the National Curriculum has been described as a 'curriculum for all' with all children being entitled to 'a broad, balanced and differentiated curriculum relevant to their needs' (NCC 1989: 1). However, Curriculum Guidance 2 indicated that entitlement to the curriculum does not necessarily ensure access (NCC 1989). For pupils with ASD it may be helpful to identify two aspects to entitlement. Firstly, there is the child, who has an entitlement to a 'broad and balanced' education. Secondly, there is autism, and the consequent individual learning needs that require structure, and in particular structured approaches to enable access to the curriculum. If pupils with ASD are to access the curriculum a number of key issues relating to entitlement must be considered, including progression, curriculum content and priorities, and curriculum delivery styles.

A hierarchy of learning, as in the National Curriculum, may be helpful for the majority of pupils but the idiosyncratic cognitive patterns of development in pupils with ASD mean that pupils' learning profiles will also be idiosyncratic (Jordan and Powell 1990b). Consideration has to be given therefore to identifying priority areas of learning for pupils with ASD, taking into account their individual learning needs. Entitlement may be enabled if we view the whole curriculum as a vehicle for addressing individual areas of need, for example providing a means of developing social and personal understanding (Rose 1998, Rose and Howley 2001). In addition, individual learning needs have direct implications for how pupils with ASD are taught. Curriculum delivery, or teaching styles, need to take into account preferred learning styles. If we take this view, the curriculum can be seen to provide the breadth and balance to which pupils are entitled, while Structured Teaching offers an approach to delivering the curriculum that takes into account the learning styles of pupils with ASD.

Curriculum content

The notion of entitlement has been strengthened in the current National Curriculum with key principles, including values, aims and purposes, underpinning the school curriculum and a statutory statement relating to inclusion (DfEE/QCA 1999a, b). The inclusion statement emphasises that 'an entitlement to learning must be an entitlement for all pupils' and schools should provide 'effective learning opportunities for all pupils' (DfEE/QCA 1999a: 30, 1999b: 32). Reference is made to individual and specific needs that may be met by the provision of a flexible approach to the curriculum that takes into account the needs of individuals. This is helpful to those concerned with addressing the individual needs of pupils with ASD. For example teachers can modify programmes of study in order to provide all pupils with 'relevant' and 'appropriately challenging' work and may choose 'knowledge, skills and understanding from earlier or later Key Stages so that individual pupils can make progress and show what they can achieve'. In addition schools are able to 'provide other curriculum opportunities outside the National Curriculum to meet the needs of individuals or groups of pupils such as speech and language therapy . . .' (DfEE/QCA 1999a: 30). Clearly this stance is beneficial to those involved in educating pupils with ASD and allows for greater flexibility to meet individual needs.

Key skills and thinking skills are key features embedded within the curriculum. The key skills of communication, working with others, improving own learning and performance and problem solving are particularly relevant for pupils with ASD as these are frequently priority areas of learning. In addition, the inclusion of thinking skills in the National Curriculum focuses on 'learning how to learn'. The need for enabling pupils with ASD to 'learn how to learn' was identified by Jordan and Powell (1990b) who suggest that 'problem solving can be seen as a key teaching resource in which the cognitive difficulties associated with autism are both most readily apparent and most accessible for remediation' (140). Clearly the promotion of key skills and thinking skills within the National Curriculum is entirely appropriate for pupils with ASD – there still remains the question of how to do it!

Entitlement for pupils with ASD raises further questions in relation to curriculum content not least 'What is an appropriate curriculum for pupils with ASD?' Pupils with ASD have specific learning needs and many have additional learning difficulties that inevitably lead to questions about what entitlement should mean in terms of curriculum content. These issues are critical to the debate surrounding curriculum and pupils with ASD and interested readers will find many references to the topic (e.g. Association of Head Teachers of Autistic Children and Adults (AHTACA) 1986, Jordan and Powell 1990a, b, 1995, Powell 2000). The focus of this book, however, is not to debate the appropriateness of specific curriculum content, rather to provide illustrative examples of how the curriculum can be taught more effectively.

Curriculum delivery

Entitlement for pupils with ASD raises equally important questions about the ways in which the curriculum is taught. Issues relating to delivery of the curriculum were, to a limited degree, addressed in the review of the National Curriculum in 1995 where some provision was made for pupils with special educational needs. The revised National Curriculum (DfE 1995) intended to provide teachers with 'greater flexibility to respond to the needs of pupils with identified special educational needs' (v), with statements relating to access for each subject. For example, for each subject area 'appropriate provision should be made for pupils who need to use means of communication other than speech, including computers, technological aids, signing, symbols or lip-reading' (DfE 1995: 1). This is clearly applicable to pupils with ASD who may use alternative and augmentative means of communication such as the 'Picture Exchange Communication System' (PECs) (Bondy and Frost 1994) or other visual modes of communication (Watson *et al.* 1989).

The current National Curriculum has developed the concept of access and identifies three 'principles for inclusion' that are central to the full participation of pupils with special educational needs:

- setting suitable learning challenges
- responding to pupils' diverse learning needs
- overcoming potential barriers to learning and assessment for individuals and groups of pupils.

(DfEE/QCA 1999a: 30–6, 1999b: 32–8)

Examples are provided to indicate how schools should respond to these principles. For example, in responding to diverse learning needs teachers should use 'teaching approaches appropriate to different learning styles' (DfEE/QCA 1999a: 32, 1999b: 34). This is further emphasised in the statutory guidance on inclusive schooling (DfES 2001a). These principles lead to greater flexibility and take into account the different learning styles of individual pupils in order to enable more effective curriculum participation for all pupils.

If pupils with ASD are to be successfully included it is essential that their learning needs and styles are recognised. The National Curriculum now paves the way for teachers to adopt a more flexible approach to the curriculum in relation to both appropriateness of content and methods of delivery. It is suggested in this book that for many pupils with ASD, more effective teaching can be achieved by the introduction of visual structure that takes into account individual strengths and preferred learning styles. Our intentions, in illustrating the use of Structured Teaching, lie with identifying effective ways of delivering the curriculum to maximise understanding for pupils with ASD.

Acknowledgement of different priorities within the curriculum at different times is essential. The needs of pupils with ASD will vary over time and the provision of an appropriate curriculum will need to be considered regularly. However, whatever the priorities for an individual pupil at a particular time, it remains essential to ensure that the curriculum is delivered in a meaningful way. Pupils with ASD require consistent approaches to both teaching and learning if they are to make meaningful progress. Recognition of the different learning needs of individuals with ASD, and the need for addressing teaching and learning styles, has led to an increase in guidance on teaching pupils with ASD (e.g. DfES 2001a, c, 2002). The move towards greater flexibility in terms of our approach to the curriculum might lead to pupils working at different levels across different aspects of the curriculum, at the same time benefiting from a consistent approach to all of his/her learning. The use of Structured Teaching is one approach to developing consistency in teaching strategies that is adaptable to differing curriculum requirements and may lead to more meaningful curriculum access for individual pupils.

The learning needs and styles of pupils with ASD: challenges to accessing the curriculum

Pupils with ASD have a range of varying needs arising from individual and idiosyncratic developmental and cognitive profiles. The notion of 'exceptional' and 'individual' needs identified by Norwich (1996) is helpful when considering the needs of pupils with ASD, and in particular, ways of teaching to increase understanding. For pupils with ASD, it is essential to identify both 'exceptional' and 'individual' needs in order to devise more successful methods of teaching. Individual pupils may present very different needs both from their peers who do not have ASD (exceptional needs, arising from the characteristics of autism) and from those who do (individual needs, for example the need for individualised levels of structure). The inclusion statement in the National Curriculum also emphasises a responsibility for responding to meet individual needs. For pupils with ASD, teaching and learning styles will need to be considered, taking into account individual learning styles and need for individualised structured approaches. One of the key principles of Structured Teaching lies in assessing individual needs and providing individualised levels of structure to help pupils to learn.

Factors that impact on learning styles in pupils with ASD

The particular learning and thinking styles of pupils with ASD have been well documented (e.g. AHTACA 1986, Cumine *et al.* 1998, Grandin 1995, Jordan 1999, Jordan and Powell 1990a, Mesibov *et al.* 1997, Schopler and Mesibov 1995). In addition, some have considered the implications of the thinking styles of pupils with ASD in relation to the National Curriculum (Cumine *et al.* 1998, Jordan and Powell 1990a, b) and the curriculum for children in the early years (Cumine *et al.* 2000). A number of priority learning areas emerge that subsequently have direct implications for teaching styles and curriculum delivery. Priority learning areas are outlined below, with examples illustrating curriculum requirements that may challenge traditional teaching styles and that have implications for teaching different aspects of the curriculum. These examples are not exhaustive, rather they illustrate the range of requirements across the curriculum where pupils with ASD may face challenges in relation to access due to their particular learning characteristics, and where we need to consider how the curriculum is delivered. Aspects of Structured Teaching that may be utilised to build upon areas of

19

strength and address challenges to access are indicated. This leads, in subsequent chapters, to more in-depth consideration and illustrations of curriculum delivery using Structured Teaching. (Note: page references relate to the National Curriculum Handbooks (DfEE/QCA 1999a, b) unless otherwise stated.)

Visual cognition

Three principles for inclusion: B Responding to pupils' diverse learning needs

Teachers should take specific action to respond to pupils' diverse needs by:

3a – creating effective learning environments

3b – securing their motivation and concentration

3c – providing equality of opportunity through teaching approaches (31, 33).

Pupils with ASD will have a range of individual strengths to build upon. While the focus is often on areas of difficulty, it is important to identify individual areas of strength in order to facilitate teaching and learning. Clearly pupils will have different areas of strength upon which to build. One area of strength that may be shared by many pupils is the ability to process visual information more effectively than verbal. Grandin (1995) tells us 'I think in pictures. Words are like a second language to me'. If pupils with ASD possess good visuo-spatial skills and are visual thinkers then clearly this provides us with a useful approach to 'responding to pupils' diverse learning needs'.

Structured Teaching is based on key principles that make use of visual structure. There is an emphasis on developing meaningful learning environments in order to enable pupils to learn. Strategies are intended to address pupils' strengths and interests, with motivation as a key factor. For many pupils with ASD, the use of Structured Teaching principles to deliver the curriculum is one effective way of responding to their diverse learning needs.

Communication

Geography Key Stage 2 Programme of Study (PoS) 1e

In undertaking geographical enquiry, pupils should be taught to:

communicate in ways appropriate to the task and audience (112).

As all pupils with ASD have difficulties with some aspects of communication there are clearly implications for how the curriculum is delivered. The teaching and learning process relies heavily on the ability to communicate, and largely upon speaking and listening; for those pupils with ASD we must develop diverse communication systems to increase meaning and understanding. This applies to all curriculum subjects, key skills, thinking skills and all aspects of the whole curriculum.

The communication curriculum of Division TEACCH (Watson *et al.* 1989) allows us to develop visual systems to improve our communication to pupils and to improve pupils' spontaneous communication skills. This can be supported effectively through Structured Teaching techniques such as the use of visual schedules, visual instructions and individualised communication systems.

Social interaction

National Curriculum key skills: Working with others

If pupils are to work with others they must develop social skills and a growing awareness and understanding of others' needs. All subjects provide opportunities for pupils to co-operate and work effectively with others . . . (21).

As with our reliance on communication to deliver the curriculum, so we require pupils to become increasingly sophisticated in terms of their social interaction skills. The majority of the curriculum is inevitably delivered within a social context that immediately challenges access for pupils with ASD. Pupils are often faced not only with curriculum subject challenges but also with challenges arising from poorly developed social skills and understanding.

Aspects of Structured Teaching can be helpful in supporting pupils in developing an ability to work with others and can help to structure interactions. For example the physical structure and the work system can be used to support and facilitate working alongside other pupils or playing in proximity.

Imagination and flexibility in thinking

National Curriculum key skills: Creative thinking skills

These enable pupils to generate and extend ideas, to suggest hypotheses, to apply imagination, and to look for alternative innovative outcomes (22).

Citizenship Key Stage 4 PoS 3c

In developing skills of participation and responsible action pupils should be taught to:

reflect on the process of participating (186).

Many pupils with ASD will experience difficulties in applying their knowledge in different contexts and generalising their learning. Pupils are often rigid in their behaviour and/or thinking and lack the degree of flexibility required to fully access all aspects of the curriculum. Repetitive behaviours and preferred interests may dominate their thinking, thus restricting access to a broader curriculum. In addition the tendency to remember events or facts without linking their memories to other events and facts exacerbates their poor generalisation skills. The ability to reflect upon curriculum content and their learning is impaired.

Many aspects of Structured Teaching are aimed at developing flexibility thus allowing the pupil to engage in a wider range of activities in varying contexts. The use of schedules may lead to greater flexibility for some pupils and additional visual information, individualised for each pupil's needs, can encourage pupils to make choices, develop more flexible ways of learning and apply their knowledge and understanding in different contexts. Visual information can be helpful in supporting pupils to begin to make guesses and to identify alternative outcomes to problems. Visual cues and structure may also be helpful in supporting and encouraging pupils to predict outcomes and to reflect upon what they have done and learnt.

Attention

Early Learning Goals: Personal, social and emotional development

Maintain attention, concentrate, and sit quietly when appropriate (DfEE/QCA 2000a: 32)

Pupils with ASD are often described by teachers as being unable to pay attention in lessons, yet at the same time will be overly attentive to some features in the environment. Some pupils will be distracted by sensory stimuli and are consequently unable to attend to the lesson. Frith (1989) describes individuals with ASD as having weak 'central coherence' in that they are often not able to see a 'whole picture' but attend to the parts that make up that picture. She suggests that they show selective attention, often attending to idiosyncratic stimuli as they are more meaningful for them. Mesibov *et al.* (1997) suggest that 'meaningfulness and salience for them is typically a more narrow and circumscribed aspect of the environment than for normally developing people' (72). This has significant implications for accessing the curriculum as pupils will often not be focusing on what the teacher requires them to focus on.

The visual emphasis of Structured Teaching approaches can be particularly helpful in enabling pupils with ASD to attend to relevant aspects of a lesson. Mesibov *et al.* (1997) suggest that individuals with ASD can attend to relevant cues when explicitly required to. The requirement to attend to relevant aspects of a particular lesson can often be made more explicit by visual clarification.

Sequencing

Physical Education Key Stage 3 PoS 8a

Gymnastic activities: Pupils should be taught to:

create and perform complex sequences on the floor and using apparatus (177).

Many pupils with ASD have difficulties following or devising sequences. Some individuals may have difficulty remembering everyday sequences, such as the sequence for dressing or cleaning teeth. Many pupils will have difficulties recalling more complex sequences in order to complete an activity, for example carrying out sequences of movements during physical education lessons focusing on ways of travelling. This will have implications across the range of curriculum subjects.

Visual information can be introduced to help pupils begin to follow and understand sequences, beginning with everyday simple sequences and developing more sophisticated sequencing abilities across the curriculum. Such structure will include for example the use of visual instructions that show a required sequence. Later this can be modified to enable the pupil to begin to construct sequences within the visual structure provided.

Organisation, planning and problem solving

National Curriculum key skills: Problem solving

The key skills of problem solving involves pupils developing the skills and strategies that will help them to solve the problems they face in learning and in life. Problem solving includes the skills of identifying and understanding a problem, planning ways to solve a problem, monitoring progress in tackling a problem and reviewing solutions to problems (21).

Planning, teaching and assessing the curriculum for pupils with learning difficulties – Key skills: organisation and study skills

Organisation and study skills may be taught at each key stage and in all subjects (15).

Many pupils with ASD show difficulties with cognitive activities such as organisation and planning and frequently do not learn from making mistakes (Ozonoff *et al.* 1991, Prior and Hoffman 1990). Ozonoff (1995) identifies such cognitive variables as executive functions, mediated by the frontal lobes of the brain. Cumine *et al* (1998) suggest that this has a number of implications for planning, self-monitoring, behaviour and flexibility. Poor executive function may help us to understand the difficulties pupils have with organisation and problem solving and may also explain inflexibility, rigidity and impulsivity. Jordan and Powell (1990a, b) place some emphasis on the need for pupils with ASD to develop problem-solving strategies and suggest that pupils will need 'specific teaching to learn and think effectively'.

Aspects of visual information may be helpful in developing some of the cognitive features identified, partly by compensating for poor abilities to organise, plan and solve problems, but also ultimately enabling some pupils to develop strategies to become more effective learners and to begin to generalise their learning. Providing visual information, at varying levels, may enable some pupils to organise themselves and the way they approach tasks, to begin to make decisions, to make choices and prioritise and to solve problems.

Motivation

Early Learning Goals: Personal, social and emotional development

Continue to be interested in, excited and motivated to learn (DfEE/QCA 2000a: 32).

PSHE and Citizenship: Key Stage 1 5b

During the Key Stage, pupils should be taught the knowledge, skills and understanding . . . through opportunities to:

feel positive about themselves (138).

Many pupils with ASD are motivated by very different aspects compared to other pupils. The foundation for motivation in schools lies traditionally within a social context and culture. Social motivation has a large role to play for most pupils who may for example respond well to verbal praise in front of peers or to competition. The social deficit in ASD often means however that pupils are not so motivated by social 'rewards' and teachers need to find other forms of motivation. This particular aspect is not a specific curriculum subject issue but is all-encompassing and will have implications across the whole curriculum.

The Structured Teaching approach places great emphasis on identifying factors that motivate pupils with ASD and then ensuring that such motivation is provided within a structure that is understood by the individual pupil. Areas of interest may be encouraged in order to motivate pupils to tackle areas of weakness, for example using a young child's interest in trains to develop early number skills. By incorporating interests and motivators into an overall visual structure pupils can be encouraged to take part in curriculum activities that they might usually resist and raise their self-esteem.

Conclusion

There are many curriculum requirements that consequently pose challenges to access for pupils with ASD, as a direct result of their individual learning characteristics. However, while these characteristics may pose challenges, they are frequently priority areas of learning for pupils. The National Curriculum, as part of the whole curriculum, provides a breadth of curriculum opportunities for developing knowledge, understanding and skills in priority learning areas associated with ASD and offers many opportunities to facilitate teaching and learning for pupils with ASD. Decisions need to be made for individuals in relation to appropriate curriculum content and this is now provided for to some extent in the 'principles for inclusion' of the National Curriculum. However, for pupils with ASD to gain meaningful access to the curriculum, teaching styles must be a priority consideration. The use of Structured Teaching, linking directly to what we know about the learning styles of pupils with ASD, offers one key approach that allows us to teach the curriculum to increase meaning and understanding.

Structured Teaching is a teaching strategy for delivering the curriculum, utilising the strengths and preferred learning style of pupils with ASD. The approach is underpinned by key principles that can be applied and adapted for individuals across the curriculum. Structured Teaching provides visual structure to enable pupils to access different elements of the curriculum. Examples in subsequent chapters will illustrate how the principles of Structured Teaching are individualised to enable pupils to access curriculum subjects, key skills and other aspects of school life such as assemblies and playtimes. Readers are guided to consider the principles underpinning the examples provided – there is no 'recipe' for producing structure due to the diversity of learning styles, strengths and challenges of pupils with ASD. Structured approaches must be individualised and therefore will be as different as the pupils for whom they are intended. The examples provided are intended to illustrate the flexibility of the Structured Teaching approach and the range of ways the approach can be adapted to enable individual pupils to access the curriculum.

**Physical structure:
making sense out of the classroom**

Overview

Physical structure refers to the way of arranging furniture, materials and general surroundings to add meaning and context to the environment. An effective physical structure helps to decrease the visual and auditory stimulation that can be distracting and troublesome for pupils with ASD. It can clarify expectations and activities. A clear and effective physical structure can also add to the pupil's sense that the world is neat, orderly and possible to master.

Clear visual and physical boundaries are a first priority in setting the physical structure of a classroom. These clear boundaries should define the basic organisation of the classroom and minimise auditory and visual distractions. These visual and physical boundaries allow the teacher to define basic teaching areas, such as group work, snack, play, transition, one-to-one work, independent work and whole-class learning areas.

Once the physical structure of the classroom is set, the teacher can begin establishing basic routines that allow the pupils to associate specific activities with specific places. These associations facilitate an understanding of basic classroom activities and expectations. They also make it easier for pupils to do what is expected when they are in the designated areas.

Although the classroom environment cannot be manipulated to the same extent for pupils in the mainstream, physical structure for these pupils is still important. Pupils with ASD in mainstream classrooms often have difficulty working independently so the designation and location of an independent work area is crucial. Pupils often do better if they are seated near or facing the teacher at a corner of a table, or at the end of a row of desks. It is important for them to understand clear distinctions such as where they work and where they have leisure. Department for Education and Skills (DfES) statutory guidelines also suggest some pupils benefit from a workstation in a quiet part of the classroom or even outside of it (DfES 2001a).

Physical boundaries are always important for people with ASD, whether they are in the mainstream or a specialist class. Having adequate space can help them to remain calm and focused on their work. It is important to clarify for pupils exactly where they are to be sitting or standing at all times in the classroom, especially when they are not at their desks, as lack of physical structure can result in inappropriate behaviour, for example wandering around aimlessly.

Distractions are especially problematic for pupils with ASD. Sometimes earplugs or visual barriers are important to help them focus on their assignments. Having a quiet area in the classroom (safe sanctuary) to go to can be very helpful in assisting pupils to calm down when they are becoming upset.

Improving physical structure and using routines to increase access to the curriculum

Physical structure is often the first step in increasing access to the curriculum for pupils with ASD. The inclusion statement in the National Curriculum identifies three principles for inclusion. In particular, the principles of 'responding to pupils' diverse learning needs' and 'overcoming potential barriers to learning . . . ' (DfEE/QCA 1999a, b) are critical for pupils with ASD and link directly to the focus of this chapter on the physical learning environment. For pupils with ASD, the classroom (and wider school context) may be a chaotic environment that causes anxiety and confusion, because of the frequent problems in segmenting their environment. Many pupils will need a clear, visually organised physical environment as a first step towards increasing their access to the curriculum. By structuring the physical context, pupils may be helped to understand the purpose of their environment.

The National Curriculum identifies the need to respond to individual needs by 'creating effective learning environments' (DfEE/QCA 1999a: 31, 1999b: 33). Statutory guidance for inclusive schooling recognises the need to take 'reasonable steps' to facilitate the inclusion of pupils with special educational needs in mainstream settings (DfES 2001a). Strategies are identified in this guidance that may help pupils with ASD to be included, for example the use of a workstation, that may be placed on the periphery or sometimes outside the classroom if necessary. The DfES guidance also identifies the need for structure and predictability for pupils with ASD. The creation of an effective learning environment will, for many pupils with ASD, need to start with the teacher considering the physical structure of the learning environment. Structuring the environment increases pupils' understanding of the physical structure within a learning context. Without clear physical structure, curriculum access may be limited, as pupils cannot identify the purposes of space. If these aspects are not addressed, pupils with ASD may resist activities and often present behaviour management issues. Physical structure is often then the first step in creating a structured and predictable environment, in mainstream or specialist settings, for pupils with ASD.

The following examples illustrate how we can begin to create more effective learning environments for pupils with ASD by considering different levels of physical structure: defining the purpose of space and reducing distractions within the learning environment. The examples are by no means exhaustive, but serve to illustrate different levels of structure in different contexts, taking into account individual needs. Curriculum links are also illustrated to indicate how the use of physical structure provides increased opportunities for curriculum access.

Early Learning Goal: Personal, social and emotional development

Curriculum guidance for teaching pupils in the Foundation Stage identifies personal, social and emotional development as one of the Early Learning Goals (DfEE/QCA 2000a). Goals relating to 'dispositions and attitudes' (33), 'behaviour and self-control' (39) and 'self-care' (41) are often challenging for pupils with ASD. The first step in addressing these challenges may lie within the physical structure of the learning context.

CASE STUDY
Physical structure in a nursery setting

Sam is three years old and has a diagnosis of autism and learning difficulties. He attends an integrated nursery where he is supported full time by a learning support assistant (LSA). Sam has poor understanding of the nursery environment, which his LSA feels is too chaotic and confusing for him. This environment has little meaning for Sam and consequently he spends much of his time running around, frequently engaging in his preferred activities and resisting other activities.

Some structure already exists as the nursery is divided into three areas for discrete activities. The 'red room' is used for creative play, the 'yellow room' is designated as a quieter working area with tabletop activities linked to literacy and mathematical development and the 'green room' is used to promote imaginative play and includes a home corner and dressing up clothes. Access is also available to an undercover outside area for gross motor play. Sam spends most of his time running between the rooms. When he does stop it is often in the creative play room to trickle sand through his fingers. Sam strongly resists joining activities in different areas and his LSA spends most of her time 'chasing' him and trying to get him to stop long enough to look at something with her. Despite the designation of rooms for specific types of activities, Sam requires clearer physical structure to enable him to make sense of the context.

A number of strategies are introduced to clarify the purpose of each area and to reduce Sam's running. Designated space is more clearly defined by using the furniture in the room to clearly demarcate specific areas, for example water and sand are clearly separated from the painting area by a screen (Figure 4.1). This helps to define specific areas for discrete activities and to reduce distractions.

A coloured chair is designated as Sam's in the tabletop activities room to indicate that Sam should sit, rather than run. This chair is positioned behind a small table, thus providing Sam with a small, secure area in which to work (Figure 4.2). A bookcase and screen are used to screen his view of the rest of the room, which would be highly distracting.

A carpet square identifies Sam's area to sit at carpet time. His square is currently placed on the periphery of the group, with his LSA, where Sam feels more comfortable. At snack time, a tablecloth adds an additional visual cue to help Sam to understand what is going to happen.

Elements of physical structure identify more clearly for Sam the purpose of specific areas of the room and reduce distractions. Combined with the use of basic 'first . . . then . . .' routines (see Chapter 5), physical structure is helping Sam to predict what will happen in a given area. This is critical in increasing his understanding and reducing anxiety and has a direct impact on Sam's behaviour and ability to learn. This aspect of Structured Teaching is an important first step in

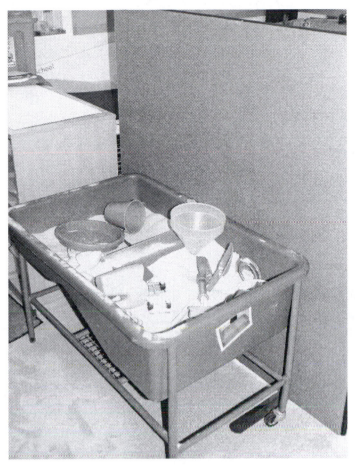

Figure 4.1: Screen used to reduce distractions in a nursery.

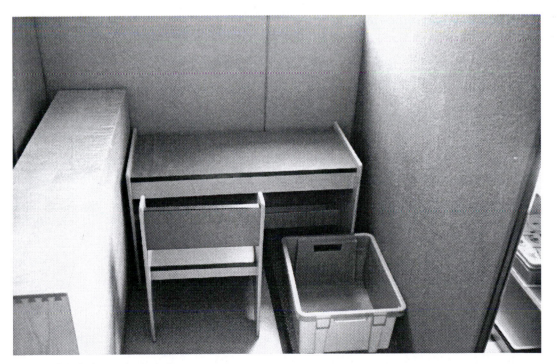

Figure 4.2: Independent work area.

addressing the learning environment for Sam as his access to the Foundation Stage curriculum will be severely restricted if he continues to run around and to resist activities. Supported by physical structure, Sam is working within the personal, social and emotional development curriculum of the Early Learning Goals (DfEE/QCA 2000a). He is being encouraged to 'feel safe and secure', 'demonstrate flexibility and adapt behaviour to different events, social situations and routines' (36) and 'maintain attention, concentrate, and sit quietly when appropriate' (32). The introduction of physical structure is coupled with the introduction of visual transition objects to further enhance Sam's understanding (see Chapter 5).

Organisation and study skills, personal and social skills

Organisation and study skills are identified as additional key skills in the curriculum guidance for teaching pupils with learning difficulties (QCA 2001b: 15). The guidance also highlights the need for pupils to learn to manage their own behaviour as part of the personal and social skills curriculum. Many pupils with ASD will have difficulties in organising themselves and consequently present challenging behaviours. For example, pupils who are easily distracted may never complete a task without multiple reminders. Adapting physical structure may help pupils to develop some of the skills required for organisation and study and as a consequence may help pupils to manage their behaviour.

CASE STUDY
Physical structure in a specialist classroom

The following example illustrates how the use of physical structure takes into account individual needs and can be used in a flexible way. Martin is 14 and is in Year 9 attending a special school for pupils with severe learning difficulties. Martin is placed in a specialist class for six pupils with autism. He spends much of his time in his base room but also goes to other classrooms for some lessons.

Martin's classroom is divided into areas that are used for designated activities through the use of screens, some furniture, mats and coloured tape. Areas are designated for independent work, group work, whole-class activities and leisure (Figure 4.3).

Martin's independent work area is in a corner of the room and faces a wall; a screen divides Martin's area from other work areas. Walls within the area are left blank to reduce distractions, although other areas of the classroom have appropriate displays. Another pupil requiring the same level of structure uses this independent area at different times to Martin. The physical structure of Martin's work area enables him to develop organisation and study skills by reducing distractions and clarifying the purpose of the workspace. This enables Martin to concentrate, to focus on relevant information, to sustain his attention for increased periods of time and to begin to work independently.

At group work times, Martin's place is indicated with his name and photograph (these are movable, so that he does not become too rigid about where he should sit). He is often given a chair at the corner of a table with a space next to him to reduce his anxieties when in close prox-

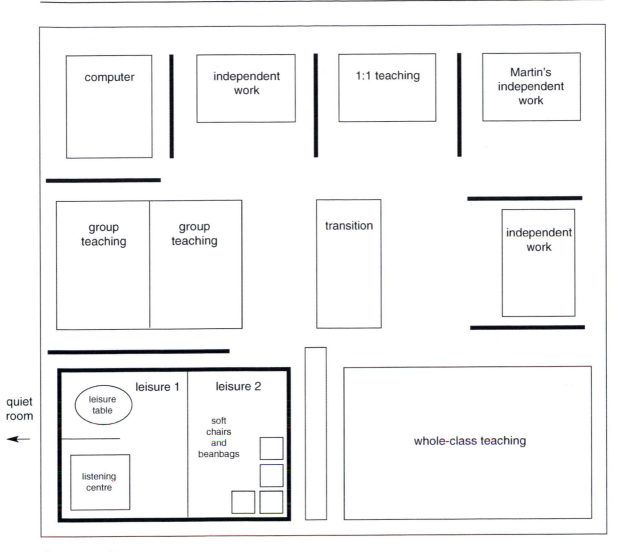

Figure 4.3: Classroom structure.

imity to others. When Martin is anxious or distracted by others in the group, he sometimes is helped by the addition of a small screen made from cardboard that stands on his table and divides his workspace from others.

During whole-class lessons, for example literacy, Martin sits on a labelled chair on the periphery of the group. The leisure area is demarcated with bookshelves, a stereo and coloured tape. A soft rug, soft chairs and a beanbag are additional visual cues indicating the purpose of the area. A 'quiet room' is available for Martin (and others) to use when he becomes upset or aggressive; he has been taught to ask to use this at appropriate times. Curriculum guidance for teaching pupils with learning difficulties identifies a number of priorities in addition to key skills and thinking skills. Among these are personal and social skills, including teaching pupils to manage their own behaviour (QCA 2001b: 15). The physical structure provided in Martin's classroom is one strategy for making it possible to teach Martin to manage his own behaviour at times of anxiety.

When Martin goes to other rooms, similar strategies are used to enable him to recognise where to sit and to help him to concentrate. For example, Martin particularly dislikes going to the art room as he finds the range of sensory experiences overwhelming. The use of physical structure in this context has been particularly important to encourage Martin to access art lessons. A small room, slightly aside from the art room, is made available to Martin to reduce some of the sensory distractions in the larger room. In addition, because of his touch sensitivity he wears rubber gloves when the lesson requires handling of media that Martin finds uncomfortable, such as papier mâché or clay. Martin has also been encouraged to increase his tolerance by introducing different textures very gradually and is beginning to join in part of the lesson in the main room, retreating into the side room when necessary. This strategy is used in conjunction with his schedule (see Chapter 5).

This level of structure helps Martin, and other pupils, to concentrate, to focus on what is relevant and reduce anxieties. Martin is more willing to join in a wider range of lessons and activities within a more meaningful physical context. Through the use of clear physical structure and the use of 'first . . . then . . .' routines (Chapter 5), Martin is able to predict what lessons and activities will be happening in particular parts of the classroom and school.

Working with others

The need to be able to work with others is identified in the National Curriculum (DfEE/QCA 1999a: 21, 1999b: 23) and in the guidance for teaching pupils with learning difficulties (QCA 2001b: 8). The nature of the social impairment in ASD inevitably leads to challenges for pupils with ASD in this area. The use of physical space and the structure of that space will be important in helping pupils to interact and work with others.

CASE STUDY
Physical structure and integration

Ricky is six years old, has ASD and learning difficulties and attends specialist provision within a school for children with a range of special educational needs. He attends the specialist class for the majority of his time, but integrates into a Year 1 class twice each week for social activities and structured play. Ricky is very active and flits from activity to activity, sometimes engaging with other children and adults. He is highly distracted, by people and events, and finds it difficult to concentrate. The level of physical structure in the classroom for Ricky is similar to that for Martin. He has an independent work area, defined by screens. The classroom also has a designated play area that includes some low-level physical apparatus, divided from the rest of the room with furniture (Figure 4.4). Two tables at the edge of the play area are used for structured play. Circle time and other class activities take place in another defined area using soft chairs and screens to reduce distractions (Figure 4.5).

Ricky's integration with peers in Year 1 is managed with one-to-one support from a LSA. At snack time, Ricky sits with a group of children at the corner of a table. A chair is labelled with Ricky's photograph and name to indicate where he should sit. As he is distracted by most events in the classroom, a small area has been defined in the classroom play area where Ricky is encouraged to join in structured play activities with two peers. A table has been designated for 'structured play' where Ricky is being encouraged to play in proximity with one peer. As Ricky

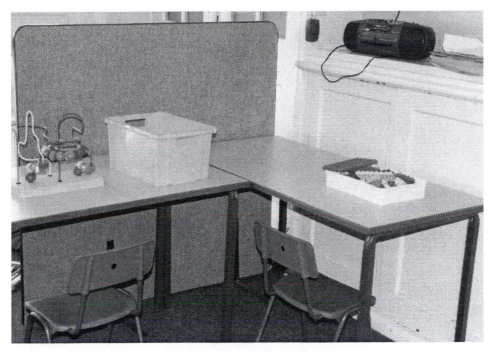

Figure 4.4: Structured play tables in a designated play area.

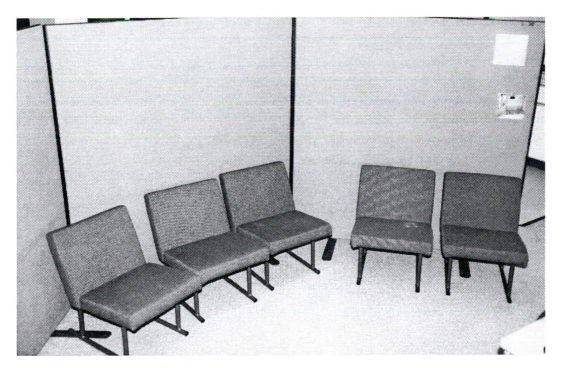

Figure 4.5: Screened area for circle times.

becomes familiar with the physical structure, he can be encouraged to play in proximity and join paired activities with peers, developing early skills relating to 'working with others'.

Physical structure at playtimes

At playtimes Ricky tends to run aimlessly around the play areas and frequently wanders into 'out of bounds' areas. The physical structure of the areas was not clearly defined and verbal reminders about where to play meant little to Ricky. He was frequently found riding a bike over the field, rather than in the allotted playground. The difficulties Ricky has at playtimes are by no means unique to him so the school has considered a number of strategies to structure the outside areas. A small section of the playground is fenced off to define a smaller area for specific activities. Cones are used to demarcate play areas and a 'road' is painted on the playground to indicate where to ride bikes. The large outside area is now divided into defined areas for discrete activities. This is helpful to Ricky, and to many other pupils, who are beginning to stay in designated areas. The reduction in running around results in greater attention to activities in each area. As the purpose of space is made clear, Ricky and his classmates are encouraged to make choices about their leisure and recreation time outdoors (QCA 2001b: 18). Lunchtime supervisors also appreciate the improved physical organisation. Their role is more clearly defined, as they are responsible for activities in each of the areas. It has been commented that Ricky, and others, are playing more rather than wandering.

Physical structure in large spaces

Similar strategies are important when defining the use of space in other large areas. For example, the school hall has three functions: PE, lunch and assembly. Ricky runs aimlessly in the large space, as do many other pupils, and catching them for a PE lesson is almost impossible! Several strategies are used to define more clearly the physical structure of the hall for each purpose. Lunchtimes are not such a problem as the space is more clearly defined by dining furniture. In addition, Ricky has a labelled chair on the corner of a table. He sits at a table at the periphery to reduce anxieties among large numbers of children.

The hall has a section that can be curtained off to create a smaller area. When the hall is used for PE, the lesson is set up in the larger space and instructions are given in the smaller, curtained off area to reduce distractions. Benches indicate where to sit while listening to instructions, before then proceeding into the larger area.

When the hall is used for assembly, a layout has been arranged in order to provide consistent cues. Benches, chairs and mats are arranged in a semi-circle and the lighting and putting out of a candle serve as additional visual cues to indicate the beginning and end of assembly. A carpet square is used to indicate where Ricky should sit during assemblies. This is placed at the end of a line as Ricky finds it difficult to sit among a large group of children. However, eventually the carpet square can be moved to different places in the line as Ricky becomes more confident in assemblies.

The physical structure and reduction of distractions is helping Ricky to develop key skills identified in the guidance for teaching pupils with learning difficulties (QCA 2001b). He is developing essential study and organisation skills as the physical structure helps him to focus and to concentrate by giving meaning to the physical context and reducing distractions. Ricky is being encouraged to stay in designated areas, rather than flitting, in order to help him to learn to work with others and to develop social skills. Simple routines reinforce Ricky's understanding of what will be happening in the classroom and what the expectations are in terms of where to sit and so on. These strategies are useful in the classroom and larger areas, helping to add meaning to the environment. The consideration of physical structure is enabling Ricky to begin to integrate with other children in another classroom, at playtimes, lunchtimes and assemblies. As with Sam and Martin, the understanding of the physical context is further supported by the use of an individualised schedule (Chapter 5).

Working alongside peers

Ricky is learning to stay in a space, to tolerate others within that space and to begin to play in proximity within a defined area. Not all pupils will require the same level of physical structure as Ricky. However, consideration of physical structure is always an important first step in enabling some pupils to share working areas and to work, as well as play, alongside their peers. The following example illustrates the adaptation of physical structure to encourage pupils to share working space.

CASE STUDY
Physical structure to encourage sharing space and to increase flexibility

Leila attends specialist provision for pupils with special educational needs, two of whom have ASD. This provision is part of a mainstream primary school. Leila is nine years old and has autism and learning difficulties. She is not easily distracted and has good concentration abilities in areas of strength. She has reasonably good understanding of the classroom context and understands the purpose of designated areas within the room. Leila has an independent work area that is adjacent to another pupil and she is able to work independently within her workspace (see Figure 6.4). Leila spends the majority of her time in the specialist classroom, but also integrates into mainstream classes for some lessons.

Integration
In the mainstream classroom, Leila has an independent work area in a corner of the classroom. The teacher has set up two working spaces within this area so that Leila is not singled out. The area is known as 'the office' and children with other special educational needs are able to use 'the office' on a rotating basis. The class teacher has found this to be a useful strategy to encourage children with poor concentration to develop independent work skills, for example during independent work in the literacy hour. 'The office' is made available at some times of the day for all children to have the opportunity to choose to work there. Thus the introduction of this physically structured space for one pupil has in fact resulted in a useful workspace for many children.

When working within a small group, a strip of coloured tape is used to define Leila's working area on the table. This has reduced Leila's tendency to spread her arms across the whole table, often upsetting her peers. This strategy is also used to define Leila's workspace in other areas, such as the food technology room. In addition, during the whole-class part of a lesson, a coloured sticker indicates Leila's space on the carpet. This has enabled Leila to begin by joining the group on the periphery. As she has become increasingly confident, the sticker is moved around so that Leila does not become too rigid about where she sits. This additional visual cue within the defined carpet area has enabled Leila to begin to sit nearer to peers and sometimes in the middle of a group. The physical structure for Leila focuses on enabling her to share space with her peers, thus laying the foundation for developing her ability to work alongside others (DfEE/QCA 1999a: 21).

Increasing participation

The physical structure of a learning environment may be helpful in enabling some pupils to participate more fully in different contexts. Pupils who are required to move from classroom to classroom may be helped by consideration of the physical structure in each classroom. The following examples illustrate how physical structure can be adapted for individual pupils in varying contexts.

CASE STUDY
Physical structure – the transition to secondary provision

David attends a specialist school for pupils with ASD. He is 11 years old. David is confident within the classroom context and is able to share a workspace, when working independently, with the use of a small, portable screen placed between him and another pupil. This is used in a similar way when he integrates into a mainstream classroom and in other classrooms in school.

Plans are being made to prepare David to make the transition to secondary provision. David will be required to move between classrooms for lessons and his working space will change from room to room. A small portable screen is being used during his visits to the new school to help him to concentrate when working next to a peer.

Despite David's understanding and confidence within the present school building, he is still sometimes distracted. He has an interest in numbers and any displays showing numbers can be highly distracting. This has been addressed by ensuring that David is positioned so that he cannot see distracting displays. Some displays are covered when they are not being used, for example a number line on the wall is covered unless it is time for numeracy. Similar strategies can be used in David's new provision. He is also being encouraged to recognise when he is becoming distracted and to place his screen on the desk top to help him to concentrate.

The level of physical structure provided for David has to be adapted for the new school context to enable him to continue to develop his ability to sustain concentration and attention. The use of small, portable screens can be helpful in a wide variety of classroom contexts, including science labs and technology rooms.

CASE STUDY
Physical structure in mainstream primary settings

Some pupils with ASD attend mainstream schools where it is not always straightforward to adapt physical structure. Nevertheless, it will be essential to consider physical aspects of the environment, to increase meaning, when necessary. Sarah is nine years old and has a diagnosis of ASD. She attends her local primary school and is supported in Year 4 by a LSA for 75 per cent of lessons. Sarah is generally confident and independent in the classroom and has good understanding of the physical context. She is able to work independently alongside another pupil and with groups of pupils, with some support from a LSA. While Sarah does not require major alterations or adaptations within the physical space, some issues have been addressed. She uses a desk mat to define her working surface as she becomes distressed if other pupils 'invade' her space. Sarah's sensory sensitivity means that she is sometimes distracted by sounds in the classroom, including the ticking of the clock and the hum of the overhead projector. Sarah always works well away from the clock and is positioned away from the projector when it is used. The teacher also ensures that Sarah has a copy of the projected image to help focus her attention on what is relevant.

CASE STUDY
Physical structure in mainstream secondary settings

Adam is 15 years old and has Asperger Syndrome. He attends a local mainstream secondary school and is studying for GCSEs. Adam has a number of strengths in particular curriculum areas, but despite his good understanding of the physical context in primary school, has had difficulties with coping with the number of transitions in a secondary school setting. For example teachers allocated seating to pupils each half term and Adam would be unsure where to sit in different classrooms, resulting in anxiety on entering rooms and subsequently at the start of each lesson. It was agreed that Adam could be allocated a consistent place in each classroom, normally in the corner at the front, which he preferred as he could leave easily if necessary. (It had already been agreed with staff that Adam should be allowed to leave lessons and return to the learning support base when feeling anxious.) Adam is now provided with seating plans for each half term, indicating his place in relation to the rest of the class (Figure 4.6).

Additional visual information also provides Adam with the structure he needs to alleviate his anxieties (Chapter 7). The combination of knowing he can leave, together with the seating plan alleviates Adam's anxieties to the point where he now stays for most lessons. Adam also experiences sensory disturbance and finds some sounds painful. The school bell, indicating ends of lessons, caused Adam great anxiety as the sound was painful to him. He spent most of his lessons worrying about when the bell would ring rather than focusing on the lesson content. Adam now has a timer, which he sets at the start of each lesson to indicate a five-minute warning that the bell will soon ring. This allows Adam time to put in earplugs to reduce the painful sensation he experiences.

Consideration has also been given to physical structure during examination periods. Adam

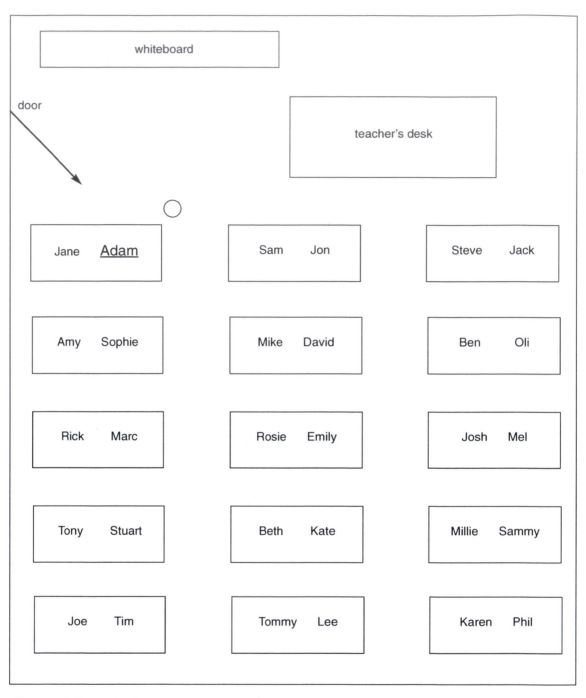

Figure 4.6: Example of seating plan provided for Adam.

becomes very anxious about sitting in the large gymnasium with many students and this leads to panic attacks before or during the exam. Adam is therefore allowed to sit all exams in the learning support base with a smaller number of pupils. At these times he is allowed to wear his earplugs to reduce background noise that he finds distracting in a quiet environment. In addition, Adam's noise sensitivity was taken into account when deciding on an appropriate context for his work experience: hence he was placed in a local library where background noise is minimal.

Another area that caused Adam discomfort and anxiety was queuing for a cafeteria style lunch and eating in the large dining area. Sensory stimulation increased Adam's anxiety in the dining hall, including noise levels and food smells. This has caused Adam to sometimes skip lunch rather than face this stressful context. Although it is not easy to alter the physical structure of the dining area, several strategies have helped Adam to adjust to this context. Adam makes his lunch choice in advance of lunchtime so that his meal can be kept hot. He is then allowed to go to the dining area at the end of the last sitting when he can stand near to the end of the queue, which he finds more comfortable. He is allowed to use his earplugs when the noise becomes too difficult for him to cope. Adam is allowed to sit in the same seat, at the periphery of the eating area. This is indicated with a 'reserved' label, as used for visitors and others at lunchtimes. When he is feeling most stressed, Adam is allowed to take his lunch to his base room. These strategies enable Adam to begin to fully participate in what is potentially for him a stressful activity.

Conclusion

All schools should be working to overcome potential barriers to learning in order to provide opportunities for pupils to access the curriculum. For pupils with ASD, some of the first potential barriers to learning might include:

- lack of understanding of the purpose of the environment or physical context
- distractibility within the physical context
- difficulties identifying personal space and sharing space
- sensory over-stimulation.

These challenges can be addressed, in varying ways, by considering the first level of Structured Teaching, taking into account individual learning needs. By addressing the physical structure and introducing basic routines, pupils with ASD can be helped to make more sense of the physical environment and to develop their concentration and attention. This chapter has illustrated how the clarification of physical structure can increase access to the curriculum in several ways (Table 4.1).

The National Curriculum states that teachers should 'plan for pupils' full participation in learning and in physical and practical activities' and that one strategy for achieving this may include adaptation of the environment (DfEE/QCA 1999a: 34, 1999b: 36). Physical structure gives meaning to the environment and is the important first step in helping pupils with ASD to fully participate and access the curriculum. Requirements relating to physical structure will vary among individual pupils and careful assessment of needs informs levels of physical structure necessary for individuals. Pupils who gain greater understanding of the physical learning environment may be enabled to participate more fully.

While the physical structure provided for a pupil with ASD is an important first step to helping them to access the curriculum, further strategies including schedules, work systems and visual information, may enhance pupil participation. Subsequent chapters build upon the foundations of physical structure to further enhance pupils' access to the full curriculum.

Table 4.1: Access to the curriculum through clarification of physical structure.

Curriculum area	Physical structure can promote
Early Learning Goal: Personal, social and emotional development	• Positive dispositions and attitudes, behaviour, self-control and self-care • Safety and security, flexibility and adapting behaviour to different events, social situations and routines • Attention, concentration • Sitting quietly when appropriate
National Curriculum: Key skills	• Working with others
Planning, teaching and assessing the curriculum for pupils with learning difficulties: Developing skills	• Organisation and study skills • Personal and social skills, managing own behaviour

5 Visual schedules: what's going on?

Overview

Daily schedules provide visual cues that tell pupils what activities will occur during the day and in what sequence. These cues focus pupils' attention on their daily responsibilities and also allow them to predict and understand what will be happening to them and in what sequence. Daily schedules can be developed at any level to match a pupil's understanding. The most common types of schedules are objects, written words with icons, pictures or photograph cards, and written schedules. The important priority is for pupils to understand their schedules so that they can use them to move from activity to activity independently.

There are several aspects of schedules that must be considered and adapted for individual pupils. First is the level of the schedule, which has already been described (i.e. objects, pictures, words etc.). Second is the length. Possible schedules that can be presented to individual pupils include single items, three or four activities at a time, a half day, or a full day. The questions to ask are can the pupil follow a sequence of activities using a visual cue and does the pupil understand a 'first . . . then . . .' sequence. If he understands these concepts, then a schedule can contain more than one item at a time.

The way in which a pupil with autism uses the schedule is also important. This active involvement can be an effective activity that keeps the child engaged in classroom responsibilities and also provides a visual message to show the pupil that progress is being made and what other activities will take place. Some pupils take their schedule words, pictures, or objects to the next activity and place them on a matching word, picture, or object. Others might turn over their schedule card in conjunction with the activity, cross it off, or place a check mark next to it on their paper. The important priority is that there is a routine method for using the schedule so that the pupil is actively engaged as he proceeds from activity to activity. The routine of checking the schedule provides the consistency pupils need and leads to greater flexibility in relation to the content of the schedule. Routine ways of checking schedules are taught, taking into account individual needs and cultural factors. Frequently pupils are taught to follow a left to right or top to bottom schedule, reinforcing reading direction. However, pupils may also be taught to follow their schedules from right to left if that is the reading direction they are most familiar with or are using. It may be important to check with a pupil's family before deciding on the routine as they may have preferences depending upon their situation.

The location of the pupil's schedule is another important consideration. For pupils with severe autism and severe learning difficulties, the teacher might bring the schedule to them so that they do not get confused by going first to their schedule and then later to an activity. For other pupils, there will probably be a transition area on the table or a wall where the pupil goes to find out what activity is next. The teacher often uses a transition card, usually displaying the pupil's name, when it is time for a transition. The pupil takes the name card, goes to the transition area where the schedule is kept, and then proceeds to the next activity as indicated on the schedule.

For some pupils the schedule can be portable, such as a clipboard indicating the daily activities or a regular daily calendar listing the sequence of activities. Portable schedules will typically be used by more capable pupils in mainstream settings or for pupils integrating into other classes or schools. These schedules allow pupils to understand exactly what will be expected throughout the day and to move from activity to activity independently.

Daily schedules help pupils to increase their flexibility. Schedules can be used to prepare pupils for changes and for 'surprises'. When pupils can see their schedules and consequently understand the teacher's expectations, then changes, when necessary, are also clear to them and much less anxiety provoking.

Using schedules to increase access to the curriculum

The principle of using schedules, at whatever level, can lead to wider curriculum access in a number of ways. The concept of a schedule is not new to schools, indeed school life relies upon the timetable in order for pupils and adults to know what is happening at a given time. However, frequently pupils with ASD will find it difficult to follow the general class timetable and therefore require individualised schedules or timetables.

Often pupils with ASD do not access all areas of the curriculum due to their lack of understanding of what is expected, for example they 'have difficulty in making sense of quite ordinary events and may not be able to display or express their confusion' (Jordan and Powell 1990a). This may lead to difficulties in behaviour. Some pupils may actively resist some, or even most, of the activities that occur within a school day. Some pupils ask repetitive questions about what is going to happen and become increasingly anxious, their ability to focus on the current activity being impeded by their worries about what might, or might not, be happening later. Often pupils are unable to predict the timetable of events, to anticipate and therefore to prepare for activities, or do not cope when changes are made to their routine. This applies to all aspects of the curriculum. These 'potential barriers to learning' (DfEE/QCA 1999a: 33, 1999b: 35) may mean that 'reasonable steps' need to be taken to facilitate the inclusion of pupils with ASD (DfES 2001a). The DfES statutory guidance identifies the use of visual timetables as one strategy for developing structure and predictability for pupils. Individual schedules can provide pupils with an understanding of the sequence of activities within a school day. Schedules can increase curriculum access by providing information in a way that the pupil understands, thus reducing confusion and encouraging access to a wider range of activities. The use of an individual schedule may help to increase wider curriculum access by:

- improving communication from teachers to pupils
- improving understanding of what will happen, when and where
- improving the ability to make the transition from lesson to lesson
- improving the ability to follow a timetable
- reducing anxiety
- increasing flexibility and the range of activities a pupil accesses.

Curriculum access depends on developing understanding so that the school timetable becomes more meaningful. It should be noted here that schedules are just one strategy for promoting wider curriculum access. Schedules do not promote greater understanding of lesson content, nor explain how to complete activities, but are critical for improving understanding of what goes on at school. After considering the physical environment, the schedule is often the next step to widening access, participation and understanding.

Schedules are always individualised according to pupils' individual needs and cognitive abilities, thus they can be adapted for individual pupils in a variety of settings. The following examples reflect the range of schedules and how they can be used to increase curriculum access at different cognitive levels. Curriculum links are identified for each example to illustrate how the use of schedules can facilitate access to the curriculum. These examples are not intended to be exhaustive, rather to illustrate the principles underpinning the approach and the ways in which these help pupils to access different aspects of the curriculum.

While examples of specific types of schedules are provided to illustrate particular curriculum links, it should be remembered that all levels of schedule can be used in relation to the same curriculum area. For example, the development of aspects of personal and social skills is illustrated through the use of a photograph schedule (see Ricky's case study). This could equally be addressed for another pupil using an object, picture or word schedule. The level of schedule used will depend upon individual developmental and cognitive abilities. Careful assessment of understanding determines the level of schedule that provides most independence; assessment is then ongoing in order to determine when pupils are ready to move to a different level of schedule. The guiding principle should be to identify the level of schedule that is most likely to increase understanding and independence and to use the schedule, at whatever level, as a strategy for accessing the breadth of the curriculum.

Transition objects

Transition objects may be the first visual cues used to help add meaning and increase understanding for some pupils with ASD. Functional objects can be used in different ways: a child may be given an object to indicate the next activity, and that object is then used as part of the activity, for example a cup indicates snack time and the child has his drink poured into his 'transition' cup. Alternatively objects of reference can be used to indicate transition, but not used as part of the activity; for example a cup indicates snack, but when the pupil arrives at the snack area, he places the cup in a 'destination' box and has a different cup to use during snack. Mini objects and parts of objects can also be used on the schedule, as long as they are meaningful to the pupil. Finally, objects may be used that are not necessarily functional or related to the activity they indicate, for example a plastic token used to indicate break time. Assessment of an individual pupil's understanding, taking into account developmental and cognitive ability, is crucial for establishing which level of object cue is appropriate. Some pupils will need to actually use their transition object during the activity in order to gain understanding of cause and effect. Others will understand that their object represents an activity without actually using it. If a pupil understands this final type of object cue, he may well be ready to begin using a combined object/picture schedule.

Some pupils with ASD have difficulties moving from one activity to another, partly due to lack of understanding about what is expected. Consequently, the pupil may resist joining any activities or may be reluctant to move from one of his preferred activities. This often causes great anxiety and behaviour that can be difficult to manage and results in restricted experience of the curriculum. Children who do not understand about the activities in a nursery setting for example, will not feel confident and may well not be motivated to join in with any activity other than their preferred one.

The use of an object schedule is one strategy for increasing curriculum access. For example, objects can be used to teach a young child about what is happening; this links directly to the Foundation Stage Early Learning Goal of personal, social and emotional development (DfEE/QCA 2000a: 28–43).

Early Learning Goal: Personal, social and emotional development

Curriculum guidance for the Foundation Stage identifies personal, social and emotional development as one of the Early Learning Goals. Learning in this area includes 'children developing a positive disposition to learn' (DfEE/QCA 2000a: 29) and includes developing self-confidence and motivation. The use of visual structure and the development of positive routines offer a strategy for developing some of the skills identified in this area of learning.

Objects are often the first level of visual information that can be used to enhance the meaning of an activity, increase understanding and help pupils to make the transition from one activity to another. This is often a first step towards increasing wider curricular access as clearly pupils cannot access the curriculum until they can make transitions without anxiety and can join a wider range of activities, rather than only pursuing their own preferred activities. Once a pupil understands that objects represent activities and events and that he can finish one activity and move on to the next, he then has increased opportunities for access. The following example illustrates how objects are used to help a pupil in the early years to understand what activity is going to occur.

CASE STUDY
Transition objects

Sam is three years old and has a diagnosis of autism and learning difficulties. He attends an integrated nursery where he is supported full time by a LSA. Sam has limited comprehension of verbal and non-verbal language but is beginning to respond to single words. Sam has poor understanding of the nursery environment, which his LSA feels he finds too chaotic and confusing. Consequently, Sam tends to seek out his favourite activity, the sand tray, where he engages in repetitive actions sprinkling sand through his fingers and trickling it onto the floor. If Sam is encouraged to join another activity he becomes agitated, putting his fingers in his ears and humming. Sam is severely restricted in his access to Foundation Stage curriculum areas. He will sometimes join in snack, scribble with felt pens and look at a book in the book corner.

One of Sam's immediate targets on his individual education plan (IEP) is to go to, and join in, an activity when directed. This links closely to the Foundation Stage curriculum and Early Learning Goals relating to personal, social and emotional development and he is being encouraged, through the use of transition objects, to 'have a positive approach to new experiences' and to 'be confident to try new activities . . .' (DfEE/QCA 2000a: 32).

Sam is presented with an object for key activities in the nursery to indicate what he should be doing next. Sam's LSA has identified seven activities as initial priorities, including Sam's preferred activities (sand, books, felt pens and cup) as well as objects for three additional events (outside, toilet and home):

spade = sand
cup = snack time
coat = outside
school bag = home

mini book = book corner
toilet roll = toilet
felt pen = teaching table

The LSA presents an object to Sam to indicate what he should do; as she gives Sam the object she says one word, for example when giving him the cup she says 'snack'.

Sam's transition objects are being used to gradually encourage him to access a wider range of nursery activities by increasing understanding and reducing anxiety. When Sam understands that each object represents an activity or event, he will be introduced to a 'first . . . then . . .' schedule with two objects indicating the sequence of two activities (Figure 5.1). Sam will learn to take the first object from the left when directed, and then the second to reinforce the concept of first you need to do this, then you need to do this.

This level of visual structure enables Sam to work towards personal, social and emotional development Early Learning Goals and offers early years practitioners strategies to 'establish routines with predictable sequences of events' and to 'prepare children for change that may occur in the routine' (DfEE/QCA 2000a: 37).

Figure 5.1: 'First . . . then . . .' object schedule indicating 'first work, then snack'.

Object schedules

Once pupils understand that an object can represent an activity or event, a sequence of objects can be used to provide information about a sequence of activities. Many pupils with ASD and additional learning difficulties will not understand cause and effect. Activities in a school day may seem chaotic as the pupils have no clear understanding of sequence, i.e. **first** I do this, **then** I do that. This often means that it is difficult to engage pupils in an activity and then to move them on to another activity when the first is finished. The use of an object schedule will be a successful strategy for some pupils in relation to developing better communication from the teacher to the pupil about the sequence of activities, and in developing early thinking skills.

Communication and early thinking skills

The National Curriculum identifies communication as a key skill necessary for all areas of the curriculum (DfEE/QCA 1999a, b) and curriculum guidance for teaching pupils with learning difficulties provides guidance on developing the key skill of communication and also early thinking skills. Critical areas include 'recognising and obtaining information' (QCA 2001b: 4), 'predicting and anticipating; understanding cause and effect and linking objects, events and experiences' (QCA 2001b: 12). For pupils with ASD and learning difficulties these skills can present particular challenges. The use of a visual schedule is one strategy that begins to address these areas. The following example illustrates the use of an object schedule that improves communication between teacher and pupil, teaches the pupil to predict and follow a sequence of activities and increases access to a wider range of activities.

CASE STUDY
Object schedule

Martin is 14 and is in Year 9 attending a special school for pupils with severe learning difficulties. He is placed in a specialist class for six pupils with autism. Martin spends much of his time in his base room but also goes to other classrooms for some lessons. He is developing key skills across the curriculum, and has individual targets for communication: one of these targets is to find out what he should be doing and to respond appropriately. Guidance for planning, teaching and assessing the curriculum for pupils with learning difficulties suggests that 'the key skill of communication is fundamental to participation and achievement in all curriculum areas' (QCA 2001b: 4). Martin's object schedule improves communication from his teacher to him, thereby increasing his understanding and specifically helping him in following information. The schedule provides him with information relating to activities that will take place during the school day, enabling him to make the transition between lessons independently. Martin is also developing early thinking skills, in particular those relating to predicting and anticipating activities. He understands that objects can represent activities and has learnt to follow a sequence of up to four objects arranged in a top to bottom sequence.

Martin's schedule is set up by the teacher or LSA for the first half of the morning until break, the second part of the morning until lunch and for the afternoon (Figure 5.2). Martin is directed to 'check your timetable' and takes a transition card with his name on it, matching it to his name at the start of his schedule. He takes the first object and goes independently to the appropriate activity, matching the object to a corresponding one when he arrives at his destination.

Where appropriate, objects that relate to curriculum areas are used to indicate the activity, for example a CD to indicate an information and communication technology (ICT) lesson or a hymn book to indicate assembly. Some objects are more abstract, for example red tokens indicate break time. Martin has in the past been resistant to some areas of the curriculum. For example, he dislikes the smells and feel of some art materials. This causes him great anxiety and he would often lie on the floor and refuse

Figure 5.2: Part-day object schedule indicating: work, gardening, snack'.

47

to go to the art room. Strategies have been introduced at a sensory level, slowly building up Martin's tolerance and reducing over-stimulation and distractions (see Chapter 4), but have also been addressed through his schedule. It is important for Martin that his schedule contains activities or events that he likes. When art is included on Martin's schedule, it is always followed by one of his preferred activities (e.g. looking through magazines). This helps Martin to cope with attending art, knowing that it will end and that the next activity is one that he will enjoy once art is finished. In this way he is encouraged to attend subject lessons that previously he had resisted.

Martin can now use his schedule to enable him to go to other classrooms and areas around the school independently. As with Sam, this is an important first step to increasing access to the curriculum. Martin understands his timetable and is empowered to follow this independently. As Martin has become independent and confident in the use of his schedule, he is being encouraged to access community activities. Prior to the introduction of an object schedule, Martin would be very anxious about leaving the school building and frequently was left behind when his class went into the community. The use of an object schedule has resulted in Martin joining community activities by increasing his understanding of where he would be going and that he would return to school. Thus Martin is now 'getting to know a local area' and is beginning to use 'different facilities and amenities in the community' (QCA 2001a: 17–18).

Martin recognises logos from specific shops and places, which can also be used to support his understanding of his schedule. In addition Martin's teacher is now attaching photographs to Martin's objects as a step towards introducing his schedule in photograph form.

Through the use of his object schedule, Martin is able to recognise and obtain information and is beginning to predict and anticipate activities as he has greater understanding of what will happen, when and where. His access to the curriculum has widened as he begins to access lessons that he would otherwise resist and ventures into the community feeling more confident.

Photograph and picture schedules

Some pupils will recognise and understand photographs that can then be used to increase their understanding of the sequence of events within a school day. Schedules can also help pupils in relation to other curriculum aspects. The importance of developing personal and social skills cannot be understated for pupils with ASD. The use of schedules may, for example, be helpful for some pupils in learning to manage their own behaviour.

Personal and social skills: managing behaviour

The curriculum guidance for teaching pupils with learning difficulties identifies a number of priorities, in addition to key skills and thinking skills. One of these priorities is personal and social skills, including the need to help pupils to 'manage and moderate' their own behaviour (QCA 2001b: 15). For many pupils with ASD and additional learning difficulties, their behaviour may seem challenging to others. Frustrations arise due to poor ability to communicate and a lack of understanding of what is happening next. Pupils may develop strong interests, become obsessive and ritualistic, preferring to engage in their own interest and avoid all other activities. This can be exacerbated by a lack of understanding of sequences of activities – why give something up if you do not know when, or if, you will ever get it back? The use of a visual schedule may help pupils to better understand sequences of activities. If pupils know when they will get some time to engage in their preferred activity or interest, they may then be more willing to join in a wider range of lessons and activities. The following example illustrates how photographs are used to increase access to a wider range of activities and to help a pupil to begin to manage his own behaviour.

CASE STUDY
Photograph schedule

Ricky is six years old, has ASD and learning difficulties and attends specialist autism provision within a school for children with a range of special educational needs. He attends the specialist class for the majority of his time, but integrates into a Year 1 class twice each week for social activities and structured play. Ricky is very active and flits from activity to activity, sometimes engaging with other children or adults. Ricky has some activities that he loves, looking at books being one of these. He is very resistant to stopping his preferred activity and moving on to another, less preferred activity, sometimes becoming aggressive to others if asked to finish; consequently he has limited access to the curriculum.

Ricky was introduced to a photograph schedule in his classroom, the aim being to teach him about the sequence of events in the classroom and to encourage him to participate in a wider range of activities without becoming aggressive to others. Ricky's schedule consists of up to five photographs presented top to bottom on a board on the wall in a quiet part of the classroom (Figure 5.3). Ricky is given a transition card with his name and photograph to direct him to his schedule. He takes the top photograph and carries it to his destination, posting the photograph in a corresponding pocket near to the activity. He quickly showed that he understood the photographs, so small symbols were added to the top of each photograph in preparation for introducing a symbol schedule.

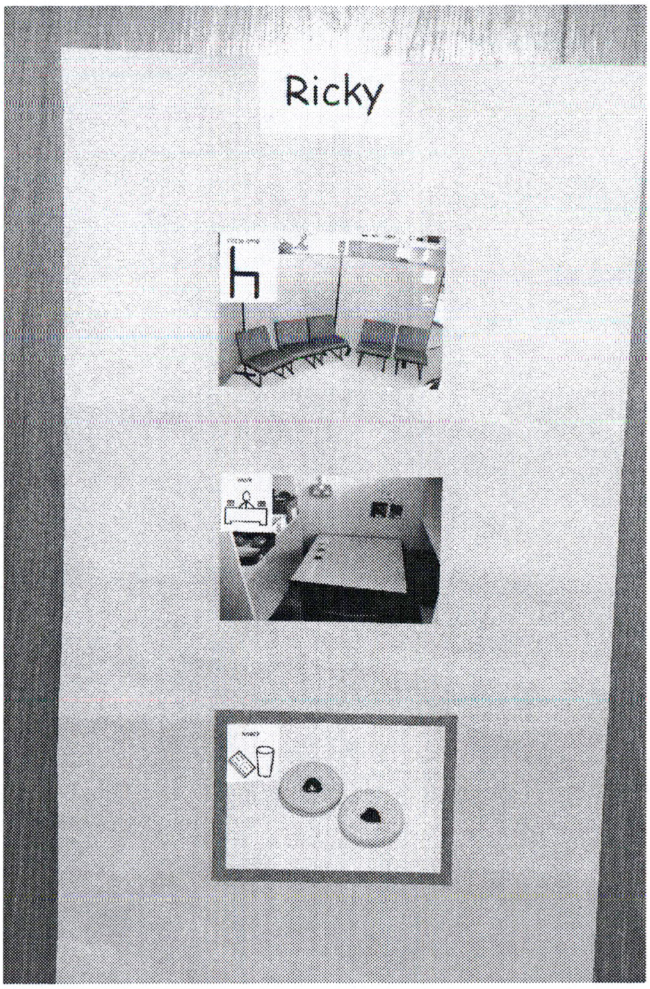

Ricky's schedule was originally set

Figure 5.3: Part-day photo schedule with added symbols.

49

up to include frequent opportunities for him to engage in his preferred activities, interspersed with short activities in other curriculum areas, thus reinforcing, for example, **first** numeracy, **then** books. Ricky's schedule has had a significant impact upon his ability to take part and focus on activities for short periods and was subsequently introduced in the Year 1 class into which he integrates. Prior to the lesson, Ricky's LSA sets up his schedule in the Year 1 classroom. It was initially felt that other children might perceive this as strange and might ridicule Ricky. However, the class teacher was delighted to find that other children began drawing and writing their own 'schedules' for the afternoon, planning activities and making decisions about how to spend their time.

Ricky is learning to use his schedule independently to encourage him to follow his timetable, rather than wander aimlessly, and to increase his understanding of the sequence of activities, thus reducing his outbursts when activities finish. The use of his schedule is one strategy for helping Ricky to gain understanding in order to begin to manage his own behaviour.

Using symbols

Some pupils will be able to recognise increasingly symbolic visual information and can use symbols to follow their timetables. Pupils who can follow longer schedules can further increase their understanding of sequences of activities and can begin to make choices and decisions. Such schedules may well address the repetitive questioning frequently heard from pupils with ASD about when events will happen. Some pupils may not remember verbal answers to their questions and may be helped by visual reminders through the use of the schedule and other visual timetables. Schedules may also indicate with whom a pupil will be working, for example which teacher; this may be helpful to those pupils who resist working with less familiar adults or who find it difficult to cope when the familiar teacher or LSA is absent. Making choices, learning to remember and working with others are all identified in the curriculum guidance for teaching pupils with learning difficulties as important skills to develop (QCA 2001b).

Working with others, early thinking skills and improving learning and performance

Working with others is identified as a key skill embedded within the National Curriculum for all pupils. The curriculum guidance for teaching pupils with learning difficulties identifies the development of social skills as one aspect of developing the ability to work with others and provides the examples of developing tolerance of others, listening and responding (QCA 2001b: 8). Many pupils with ASD find these particular skills challenging; for example working with less familiar adults or coping with changes in staff can result in strong resistance to joining in. This is one area therefore that needs to be focused upon in order to help pupils to increase their access to the curriculum, particularly where pupils are required to work with different adults for different lessons. The use of a schedule that indicates who the teacher or LSA is for particular lessons often reassures pupils with ASD; changes are no longer unpredictable as pupils are given warnings through their visual schedules.

The QCA curriculum guidance includes 'remembering' as an early thinking skill. An example of developing this skill is provided in the guidance and makes use of a 'thinking board' that is used by following symbol sequences of information (QCA 2001b: 13). This is similar to the use of a schedule, which can be used to enhance a pupil's ability to recall and follow the day's activities and lessons.

Finally, the National Curriculum includes 'improving own learning and performance' as one of the key skills pupils will need to develop (DfEE/QCA 1999a: 21, 1999b: 23). Making choices and communicating preferences are indicated as aspects of developing this skill for pupils with learning difficulties (QCA 2001b: 9). Many pupils with ASD will have difficulties when faced with making even the simplest of choices. Once pupils are familiar with and secure in the use of a schedule, choices can be incorporated in order to give opportunities to develop this particular skill. The following example illustrates the use of a symbol/word schedule to enable a pupil to work with an increasing number of staff, to improve her recall and to make simple choices.

CASE STUDY
Part-day symbol schedule

Leila attends specialist provision for pupils with special educational needs, two of whom have ASD. This provision is part of a mainstream primary school. Leila is nine years old and has autism and learning difficulties. Leila has poor short-term memory and attention span and cannot recall the sequences of activities that take place during the day. This causes her anxiety and confusion and she will frequently refuse to join in some lessons. In addition, Leila is resistant to working with less familiar adults. Consequently she often refuses to cooperate with teachers in mainstream classes and supply teachers. This means that she is unlikely to join lessons not taught by her teacher. Leila's teacher has identified this as a priority as Leila clearly needs to learn to work with a variety of people if she is to access the full range of the curriculum. Finally, Leila shows anxiety when confronted with situations that require her to make choices. Leila's schedule is being used to encourage her to become more independent in relation to transitions between lessons, to work with different adults and to become more confident about making choices.

Leila has a part-day symbol schedule consisting of up to five symbols at one time, presented from left to right on a pinboard (Figure 5.4). This was decided after consulting her parents who felt that while they were familiar with right to left text, they would rather Leila follow left to right and top to bottom information as this is what she is most likely to encounter in her everyday life

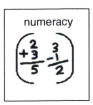   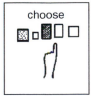

Figure 5.4: Part-day symbol/word schedule.

in the community. Hence, Leila is taught to look for information using left to right or top to bottom routines. Leila's schedule is kept in her work area in the base classroom. She takes the first symbol from her schedule and goes to the appropriate lesson, posting the symbol card into a corresponding pocket when she arrives at her destination. Symbols are often paired with a written word, which may help some pupils to subsequently follow a written schedule. The schedule can then also be used as one tool for helping some pupils to develop a sight vocabulary, by using familiar words on their schedule. This enables the pupil to learn a skill within a functional context, i.e. reading for information. Leila is working towards P6 in reading, so key words are written below each symbol (Reading P6, QCA 2001c: 31).

When Leila is scheduled to work with the teacher, a small photograph of the teacher is attached to the appropriate symbol card, thus she knows what she will be doing and who with. When a supply teacher is in the class, his or her photograph replaces the usual teacher so that Leila has some warning that she will be working with someone different. This has proved highly successful and Leila will now work with a number of people, including different LSAs and classroom helpers as long as they appear on the schedule.

When Leila integrates into mainstream classes, she takes a clipboard with a symbol schedule. A photograph of adults in the classroom she is going to is attached to the clipboard. Consequently Leila is able to integrate in the mainstream class and cooperate with different teachers. The schedule has been very reassuring for Leila. She uses it independently and is less likely to refuse to join certain lessons. Through the use of her schedule, Leila is also developing organisation and study skills, identified in the curriculum guidance for pupils with learning difficulties, by learning to manage her own time and taking responsibility for completing tasks by following her schedule (QCA 2001b: 15).

In addition, as Leila's confidence and independence have grown she is now able to make simple choices, hence 'choose' is incorporated onto her schedule. Choices that are available are indicated on a choice board and Leila is being encouraged to make choices during the school day (Figure 5.5).

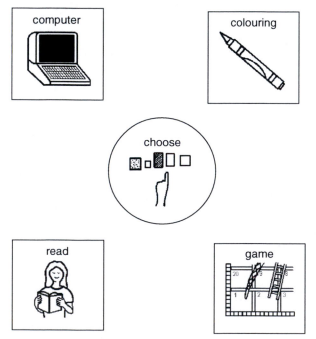

Figure 5.5: Choice board.

Making choices is an important skill, but one that pupils with ASD often find difficult. Leila is learning to make choices relating to 'leisure and recreational skills' (QCA 2001b: 18). Making simple choices at this stage, using a choice board, prepares Leila for making increasingly sophisticated choices within curricular areas at a later date.

The use of a choice board can also be an effective classroom management strategy. If the teacher does not want more than one pupil to have the same choice, only one choice card for that activity is available on the choice board. Equally, if the teacher wants to encourage two (or more) pupils to play with the same resources, two (or more) choice cards for the activity can be placed on the choice board. For example, a choice board for young children might include one picture of the train set when there is nobody to supervise two children who may fight over the train! Equally, if the teacher wants to encourage two pupils to play with the train together, and somebody is available to supervise if necessary, two train pictures can be placed on the board.

Leila's schedule helps her to develop a number of skills that are essential to developing independence and promoting participation and learning. She is learning to use a visual strategy to enable her to recall and follow sequences of activities. She is being encouraged to work with a number of adults, by warning her of any changes and enabling her to predict, and she is being given opportunities to develop the ability to make simple choices. A further example illustrates how the schedule can be extended to meet different individual learning needs and to provide opportunities to increase early thinking skills.

Decision making, reasoning and participation

The development of thinking skills is identified within the National Curriculum as being a crucial element embedded within the curriculum. All pupils need to 'know how' to learn and for pupils with ASD, 'learning how to learn' should be incorporated into all aspects of learning (Jordan and Powell 1990b). Thinking skills such as reasoning are frequently difficult for pupils with ASD and need to be addressed in all areas of the curriculum. Opportunities should be provided to encourage pupils to begin to develop their own thinking skills in relation to the problems that they will face in their everyday lives. The use of schedules may encourage pupils to develop a problem-solving approach by offering opportunities to make choices and decisions. They can also offer opportunities for pupils in specialist settings to participate in integrated activities.

CASE STUDY
All day symbol/word schedule

David attends a specialist school for pupils with ASD. He is in a Year 6 class and is preparing for the transition to secondary provision. David has good word recognition skills and although he has difficulties understanding fiction, he is able to read directions and to follow written information when accompanied with symbols. He has a number of particular interests including numbers, weather and temperature. David integrates into a local mainstream primary school for some mathematics lessons. David has an all day symbol/word schedule that is kept on a clipboard in the classroom. His schedule is set up for the day and follows a top to bottom, left to right sequence (Figure 5.6). His schedule is generated using the computer and is divided into morning and afternoon. David uses a coloured 'frame' that highlights the activity he is currently doing, moving it down to the next lesson and crossing out the lesson that has finished when it is time to move on. He does not need to carry symbol cards as he is able to remember where to go and is not likely to be distracted on the way to his destination.

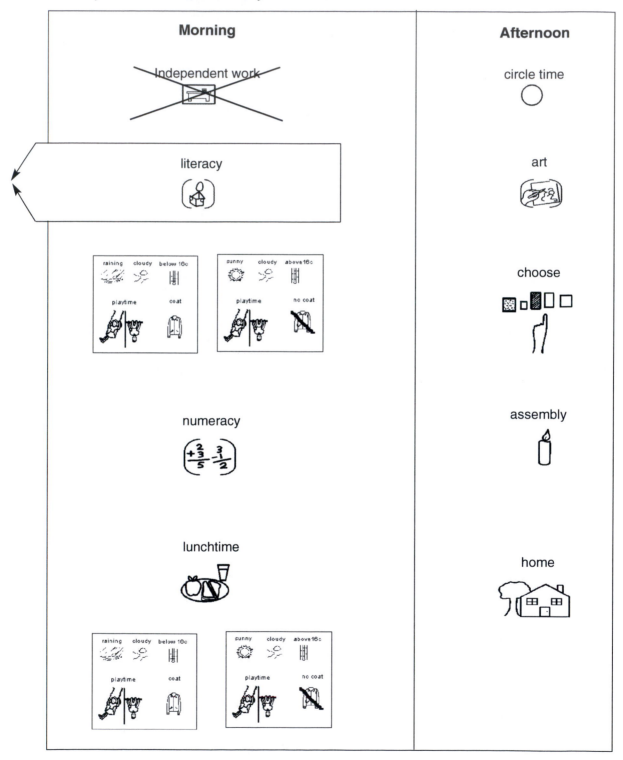

Figure 5.6: All day symbol/word schedule.

David is now able to negotiate some activities on his schedule. He is also encouraged to make decisions and choices about his day as a first step towards developing thinking skills. David's teacher prioritised making decisions as a target for David and decided to link this initially to areas of strength and interests to encourage him to become more confident in making decisions. Hence David's interest in weather was utilised to help him to make a decision about whether he would need a coat at break time or not, something that often worried him. At break times two symbols appear on the schedule: playtime with a coat and playtime without a coat. Each of the symbol cards corresponds to a weather symbol and a temperature indicator (Figure 5.7).

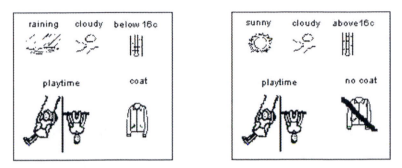

Figure 5.7: Using the schedule to encourage simple decision making at playtime.

David is encouraged to look at the weather and also look at the class temperature gauge to help him to make a decision about whether he needs to wear his coat or not. Thus the schedule indicates when the break is but also encourages David to make a decision about what he will need to wear at playtime. His schedule is helping him to make decisions by indicating alternatives at certain times of the day. David then has to find out relevant information in order for him to make his decision. This might link directly to a National Curriculum subject, in this case geography (Geography Key Stage Two: PoS 2b, DfEE/QCA 1999a: 112). Similar strategies are used to help David to make decisions about what he might need for a variety of activities and lessons; for example a choice of PE equipment for different sports is used to encourage David to select appropriate resources.

'Potential barriers to learning' could arise for pupils with ASD when integrating into a mainstream class. Increased anxiety may result in increased confusion. Learning will not necessarily generalise into a new setting and pupils may feel de-skilled in what may be a more demanding environment. The use of a schedule is one of the strategies that can be used to plan for participation in learning in the mainstream classroom.

When David integrates into a mainstream class for mathematics he takes a portable schedule in a ring binder folder that is set up with the LSA. During David's visits to his new secondary provision, the same approach is used. The need for a portable schedule is important particularly as pupils begin to move to different classes and to other facilities within the community; portable schedules can be provided in different forms including clipboards, mini whiteboards, personal organisers and ring binders. The use of a schedule is one strategy that helps David to integrate and to participate in a mainstream classroom for some lessons by alleviating his anxieties and ensuring that he understands what will be happening.

Written schedules

Written schedules are used in the same way but allow for increasing flexibility and can be presented in a wide variety of ways. These schedules may look increasingly similar to the diaries, calendars and year planners that we all use in our day-to-day lives. Some individuals with ASD use electronic organisers that incorporate their schedules. As pupils become confident in the use of their individual schedules, further strategies such as incorporating a work system (see Chapter 6) can be used to enhance the schedule in order to develop additional key skills.

Thinking skills

For many pupils with ASD, the development of thinking skills, requiring the ability to reason, enquire and evaluate, is challenging. Pupils with ASD who have average or above average abilities in some areas of the curriculum, may still have difficulties in developing these skills. The QCA curriculum guidance for teaching pupils with learning difficulties may be helpful in teaching 'early thinking skills' as a precursor to developing the more sophisticated skills indicated in the National Curriculum. For example, the QCA guidance includes 'remembering' and 'predicting' as early thinking skills (QCA 2001b: 13). The following example illustrates a written word schedule that enables a pupil to recall when events will be happening and an additional class 'diary' highlighting key events of the week.

CASE STUDY
Written schedule

Sarah is nine years old and has a diagnosis of ASD. Sarah attends her local primary school and is supported in Year 4 by a LSA for 75 per cent of lessons. Sarah has good expressive language, although this can mask her difficulties with comprehension. She has poor organisational and sequencing abilities and asks repetitive questions about the week's events, such as 'Is it swimming today? Are we going swimming? When is it swimming?' Sarah is dependent on routines and becomes anxious when changes are made to the day's activities without warning. Sarah's schedule provides opportunities for negotiation, decision making and problem solving. She is being encouraged to develop early thinking skills by using a visual diary as a reminder for key events. In addition, Sarah is learning to recognise her own anxieties and to develop strategies to reduce that anxiety.

Sarah uses a written schedule, arranged top to bottom in two columns, as a list on a clipboard that she keeps with her (Figure 5.8). Sarah follows the left-hand column of her schedule for the morning, crossing out each lesson or activity when it is finished. She then follows the right-hand column for the afternoon. Sarah's schedule helps her to understand and follow the sequence of lessons throughout the day. She is less anxious about what will be happening and copes with changes to the timetable when they are made clear on the schedule: for example playtime outside can be altered to indoor play if it is raining. Her teacher feels that the reduction in anxiety has allowed Sarah to focus on the lesson, rather than on what will be next. Sarah's schedule also

Remember:

put up my hand when I want to answer a question

Today's date _____

AM	**PM**
numeracy	science
playtime	music
literacy	?
lunchtime	home
playtime	

Figure 5.8: All day written schedule.

provides a message or reminder that she can refer to throughout the day; this is often a reminder about a behaviour that the teacher is trying to encourage.

Sarah's repetitive questioning about events has reduced as she is now able to see for herself when activities will happen. As Sarah has become confident in her use of her schedule it is possible to add a symbol (?) that indicates that something will happen but we do not know what. This will teach Sarah to cope with unscheduled activities that are part of everyday life.

In addition to her individual schedule, a class timetable has been introduced identifying key events for the week. Sarah is referred to this if she asks about events more than once. The weekly timetable incorporates symbols with words (Figure 5.9) as Sarah's anxieties regarding some weekly events lead to her becoming 'de-skilled' in terms of her reading ability. The class teacher introduced this for the whole class as she felt that other children with special educational needs might benefit from being able to see the overall weekly timetable.

Sarah's schedule, together with the class timetable, is providing a tool for Sarah to use in order to enhance her ability to remember, and predict, daily and weekly events. Sarah is asking less often about events, instead referring to the schedule or class diary as appropriate. She is beginning to develop early thinking skills that will serve as a basis from which she can continue to develop her thinking.

Figure 5.9: Weekly symbol/word timetable for class.

Increasingly complex schedules

The demands of a mainstream secondary school context are quite different from those in a primary school, including a much larger physical context, movement between classrooms and buildings, and larger numbers of teachers. Timetables may be far more complex than those experienced in a primary school. Pupils will need to solve basic everyday problems, which might mean how to find a route from one classroom to another. They will need to cooperate and work with more staff and pupils, make choices and decisions and prepare for the transition to the world of work. These demands may well lead to anxiety and frustration, resulting in inappropriate behaviour. The individual schedule will play a critical part in helping pupils to understand, and respond to, these demands.

Problem solving, personal, social and health education, work-related skills and managing behaviour

Key skills relating to problem solving 'involve pupils developing the skills and strategies that will help them to solve the problems they face in learning and life' (DfEE/QCA 1999b: 23). The individual schedule may help pupils to become more independent in solving some of their everyday challenges relating to the timetable, changes to timetables and staffing. During Key Stage 4, for example, pupils will need to be given opportunities to participate, make choices and decisions, meet and work with people and prepare for change (DfEE/QCA 1999b: 193–4). Increasingly sophisticated use of the individual schedule offers pupils with ASD one strategy within Structured Teaching for developing increasing independence in these areas. Pupils will also need to prepare for moving to college or to work (DfEE/QCA 1999b: 24). The use of a schedule will need to be adaptable to these different contexts and will be important in preparing for change. In addition, it becomes increasingly important for pupils to manage their behaviour and to behave appropriately in a wide range of contexts. In overcoming potential barriers to learning, teachers should 'help pupils to manage their behaviour' (DfEE/QCA 1999b: 37); social rules on a schedule may act as reminders of appropriate behaviour. The following example illustrates how the written schedule can be extended to enable pupils to become increasingly independent in more complex situations.

CASE STUDY
All day written schedule and student planner

Adam is 15 years old and has Asperger Syndrome. He attends a local mainstream secondary school and is studying for GCSEs. Adam has a number of strengths in particular curriculum areas but has had difficulties with coping with the number of transitions in a secondary school setting. In addition, the school operates a two-week timetable system and Adam was often unsure which week he should be following. He frequently became lost on his way to the science labs and was often late for lessons as he could not recall the layout of the building. Adam would become very anxious when late as he likes to be punctual and worries if he misses the beginning of a lesson. Adam is a typical example of a pupil who has average to above average abilities in some curriculum areas, but who has difficulties in other key areas.

Adam has a student planner that provides two timetables, A and B, for his year group like all other students (Figure 5.10). Adam's timetables have been clarified with room numbers for lessons that are held in different rooms highlighted. He also has a plan of the building that highlights key places in the same way as the timetable. A plan is provided to show the specific route

Week A	8.45a.m.		BREAK	11.00a.m.		LUNCH	1.30p.m.	2.30p.m.	
Monday	English 101 JW		K	Maths 205 DG	Learning support	H	PE (gym or field – check schedule) AS	PE (gym or field – check schedule) AS	
Tuesday	History 115 IP		A	English 101 JW		C	Science L17 AW	Science L17 AW	Learning support
Wednesday	English 116 IP		E	ICT 104 KL		N	Maths 205 DG	Maths 205 DG	Learning support
Thursday	History 115 IP	Learning support	R	Science L14 JR		U	Geography 108 DS	Art A15 MH	
Friday	English 107 IP		B	RE 108 MW	Learning support	L	PSHE 101 JW	ICT 104 KL	

Reminder: go to learning support at 8.30a.m. and 3.00p.m. every day.

Week B	8.45a.m.		BREAK	11.00a.m.		LUNCH	1.30p.m.	2.30p.m.	
Monday	Maths 206 IA		K	English 116 JW	Learning support	H	PE (gym or field – check schedule) AS	PE (gym or field – check schedule) AS	
Tuesday	RE 108 MW	Learning support	A	English 101 JW		C	Science L15 AW	Science L15 AW	Learning support
Wednesday	English 116 IP		E	Science L14 JR		N	Maths 205 DG	Maths 205 DG	Learning support
Thursday	Drama studio MH		R	Art A15 MH		U	Learning support	ICT 104 KL	
Friday	Geography 108 DS		B	History 117 IP	Learning support	L	PSHE 101 JW	ICT 104 KL	

Reminder: go to learning support at 8.30a.m. and 3.00p.m. every day.

Figure 5.10: Two-week planner timetable.

from the room he is in before 'learning support' to the support base as the routes vary between weeks A and B. The initials of teachers are also provided for each lesson so that Adam knows who the teacher will be.

Adam's student planner is inserted within a ring binder, divided into week A and week B. Adam has one week to view within his file, the second week is placed within a transparent wallet. Adam changes the week to view on Friday afternoons with the help of learning support. Each week is subdivided into a number of sections including days of the week and homework for each week. The homework section allows Adam to add any extra information he needs, for example hand-in dates and who to hand work in to. This is checked on a regular basis with learning support. Adam has recently included an additional section in which he keeps his social stories.

Adam has a written schedule for each day, which he has learnt to construct himself from the weekly timetable (Figure 5.11). Changes to the timetable are recorded on a whiteboard in learning support so Adam can make sure his schedule is accurate. His schedule also incorporates important 'notices' that serve as constant reminders to Adam. These might include reminders about which sports kit is required for PE, 'social rules' that remind him, for example, not to interrupt but to raise his hand (used in conjunction with a social story) or where to put work that is not finished. Adam finds these reminders reassuring; they reduce the need for him to constantly ask questions to seek reassurance and for the LSA to give verbal reminders that might reduce independence.

Monday	**Week A**
8.30a.m.	Learning support: check schedule for the day
8.45a.m.	English 101 (LSA: Mrs Smith)
10.30a.m.	Break: library or outside
11.00a.m.*	Maths <u>207</u> (LSA: Mrs Taylor)
11.45a.m.	Learning support – independent study time
12.15p.m.	Lunch Break: outside or learning support
1.30p.m.	PE: field, shorts, T-shirt and trainers
3.00p.m.	Learning support: check homework diary and schedule for tomorrow

Reminders:

raise my hand rather than interrupt

work that is not finished can be filed as unfinished – check with the tutor when to finish it

Figure 5.11: Written daily schedule incorporating * to show change to timetable and social rules.

Adam can make changes to his schedule as and when necessary. The learning support staff who work with him meet regularly with Adam to discuss any changes to his schedule or week, such as changes in teachers or changes to the timetable. In addition, his schedule can incorporate other important information relating to work organisation (see Chapter 6). Adam's planner and schedule are useful strategies for enabling him to become more independent, to develop problem-solving strategies, to cope with alterations to the timetable and to work with a wider number of staff by enabling him to predict who will be teaching specific lessons.

The National Curriculum for pupils in secondary schools identifies the need for offering opportunities for 'work-related learning' (DfEE/QCA 1999b: 24). Adam's school is involved in a number of initiatives to provide pupils with a range of opportunities in this area, including work experience and vocational courses at a local college of further education. Initially Adam was very anxious about participating in work-related activities but after completing several visits to workplaces he was able to complete a work experience placement in a local library. Adam took a written schedule within the diary section of a Filofax with him to the library; this gave Adam access to the range of information he would need for the placement, including his schedule, incorporating social rules and reminders about expected behaviour.

The schedule is one strategy that enables Adam to develop skills in personal, social and health education (DfEE/QCA 1999b: 190). The schedule provides meaning and security to enable Adam to 'participate', to 'make real choices and decisions' and to 'meet and work with people'. Without his schedule, Adam experiences anxiety, which then reduces his ability to participate fully in the breadth of activities provided. Adam is becoming increasingly independent through the use of his individualised planner and schedule. He is beginning to construct his daily schedule for himself by referring to his overall weekly planner.

Conclusion

Schedules are a helpful strategy to enable pupils with ASD to understand and follow the sequence of day-to-day events. When a pupil can follow a schedule this may facilitate access to a wider range of lessons and activities. The use of visual schedules is one strategy within Structured Teaching for addressing some of the needs of pupils with ASD and is an important element within the overall structure that many pupils will need. Schedules are one strategy for responding to diverse needs and providing a teaching style appropriate for pupils who are visual learners. Curricular access can be improved with the use of schedules for both understanding the sequence of lessons and developing skills embedded within the curriculum. Table 5.1 summarises aspects of access that may be facilitated through the use of schedules.

The use of individual schedules will require careful assessment, planning, monitoring and reviewing. If we are devising approaches to take into account a visual learning style, it will be necessary to assess individual pupils to establish their level of visual cognition. Planning for schedules can be incorporated into pupils' individual targets, thus ensuring that progress is monitored and reviewed. Some pupils will progress to increasingly complex schedules, others may remain at a particular level; either way, monitoring and reviewing is essential to ensure that the approach does not become stagnant. Essentially, schedules are used that are most functional and meaningful for the individual pupil; the aim is for greatest understanding and independence. It is important that all staff who work with the pupil are familiar with his schedule and how it is used to ensure consistency of approach.

Table 5.1: Access to the curriculum through use of schedules.

Curriculum area	Schedules can promote
Early Learning Goal: Personal, social and emotional development	• Positive disposition to learn • Self-confidence • Motivation • Establish routines • Prepare for change
National Curriculum:	
Key skills	• Communication • Improving own learning and performance • Working with others
Thinking skills	• Problem solving • Reasoning
Personal, social and health education (PSHE)	• Participation • Making real choices and decisions • Meeting and working with people
Planning, teaching and assessing the curriculum for pupils with learning difficulties: Developing skills	
Early thinking skills	• Recognising and obtaining information • Predicting and anticipating • Understanding cause and effect and linking objects, events and experiences • Predicting and anticipating • Learning to remember • Improving own learning and performance: making choices and communicating preferences
Daily living skills	• Community skills
Personal and social skills	• Managing own behaviour
Other aspects of the school curriculum	• Work-related learning

While schedules may go some way to helping pupils to increase their access to the curriculum, by increasing understanding of the sequence of activities and developing key skills, difficulties with organisation and sequencing may still hinder the pupil. This may include difficulties with starting and/or finishing activities, from working independently or in groups, and may lead to challenging behaviour. The next level of Structured Teaching focuses on helping pupils in getting organised within a range of learning contexts.

6 Work systems: getting organised

Overview

The individual work system gives the pupil a systematic way to approach the work that needs to be completed for each of his tasks within a lesson. It is a strategy that engages pupils with ASD, builds independence, and enables them to generalise their skills into other settings. Complementing the schedule which outlines the sequence of activities that a pupil is to follow during the day, the work system tells the pupil exactly what activity he is to do. The work system organises each pupil's work so that no matter what his level of ability he can identify what work is supposed to be done, how much work is to be completed, how to understand that he is making progress, know when he is finished, and then what happens next. The work system is an extremely important and effective way of organising individual activities to give pupils strategies for completion and an understanding of important concepts related to their work, such as when their work is finished.

Similar to schedules, there are different work systems for pupils at different levels of ability. For pupils with ASD and additional learning difficulties, the work system simply is organised from left to right. The pupil's work is placed at his left on a single tray or perhaps in individual baskets. The pupil is taught a left to right sequence and that the work is completed when everything from the left has moved to a 'finished' basket on the right. Other possible work systems require matching skills to complete tasks in a particular sequence or a written system. It is also possible to embed a work system into a schedule for pupils with good cognitive and conceptual skills.

There are several important ways to individualise work systems. One can change the visual cues or the concept of finish. For example, finish can simply mean the materials move from left to right, or are placed in a 'finished' box, or are taken to another location in the classroom which is a 'finished' area, or put back on the shelf, or checked off after they are completed. Different systems will be more or less effective with different pupils.

For the pupil included in a mainstream school, it is especially important that he can identify what work he is supposed to do, and can understand how much must be completed in a specific work period. It is also important for the pupil to be able to see that he is making progress as he works and to know when he's finished and what to do with work that is not finished. Understanding what comes after the work is also important for the transitions that pupils in mainstream schools must be able to make, particularly in secondary settings.

Using work systems to get organised

All pupils, at all ages, need to develop work, study and organisational skills in the classroom. Curriculum guidance and documentation for all pupils makes some reference to this area. For example children in the early years, in their personal, social and emotional development are encouraged to 'show increasing independence in selecting and carrying out activities', 'be confident to try new activities' and 'maintain attention, concentrate and sit quietly when appropriate' (DfEE/QCA 2000a: 32). In addition, they should learn to 'select and use activities and resources independently' (40). For primary and secondary aged pupils, the National Curriculum includes as a key skill, 'improving own learning and performance' (DfEE/QCA 1999a: 21, 1999b: 23) and pupils in secondary schools are involved in 'work-related learning' (DfEE/QCA 1999b: 24–5). In addition, curriculum guidance for pupils with learning difficulties highlights the need to develop 'organisation and study skills' (QCA 2001b: 15). Many of these aspects will inevitably require some ability to work independently.

Pupils with ASD, at any age or stage in their learning, often face particular challenges in this area due to poor organisational and sequencing skills. Confusion arises as pupils do not understand what work they are to do, how much to do, what to do with the work when it is finished and what to do next. This means they may never begin a task set, or may not know when, or how, to finish. Others will begin, but refuse to finish in the allotted time, not understanding what to do with unfinished work. This may cause extreme perseveration, leading to frustration and sometimes challenging behaviour. Sequencing difficulties may mean that a pupil completes one task of several required, but does not complete the whole set. Sometimes a pupil does not begin a task, or stops in the middle, because he has no idea how long it will last, or what will happen when it is finished. Tasks can appear to be never-ending; if a pupil has an interest or activity that he prefers, he is unlikely to give it up in order to begin something that may never end, with no idea when he might resume his preferred activity! These difficulties are found across the ability range, hence pupils with average to above average academic abilities may still have problems with organisation and completion of sequences of tasks, often spending most of their lesson trying to get organised and subsequently not completing the task.

Curriculum access relies upon pupils developing organisational skills. Pupils are encouraged from an early age to work independently and this has been emphasised for example in *The National Literacy Strategy* (DfEE 1998: 9, 12–13). However, pupils with ASD will be at a disadvantage unless teachers consider their individual needs relating to organisation and sequencing. The use of the work system, as part of a Structured Teaching approach, is one useful strategy that teachers can use to enable pupils to fully participate in curricular activities by considering:

- the learning environment
- organisation and sequencing
- motivation and concentration
- communication.

The following examples illustrate different levels of work system, how to use these to increase independent work and organisation skills, how to use work systems across the curriculum, either individually or when working as part of a group, and how to provide opportunities for communication within a work system. Discussion focuses upon organisational strategies provided by a work system. The development of appropriate learning tasks, and how to structure activities within a work system, are discussed in detail in Chapter 7.

Introducing a work system

Work systems are visually structured organisation systems to help pupils to complete tasks effectively and to understand the following:

- What work do I have to do?
- How much do I have to do?
- How do I know I am making progress, how do I know when I am finished and where do I put the work when it is complete?
- What will I do next?

These are important questions that we all need to address in our daily working lives. Many of us would find it difficult to become motivated by a task that seems never-ending and we often organise our time so that we have the answers to the above questions (for example, ironing!). Many pupils with ASD do not have access to this information and may be helped by the use of a work system that gives clear visual information relating to the above questions. The use of a work system helps pupils to develop organisational strategies that develop self-confidence, concentration and motivation and pupils may then be able to access a wider number of activities within a lesson. When introducing a work system, it will be important to ensure that the pupil learns to use a system that provides answers to the above questions. This then provides an organisational framework that may enable the pupil to access a wider range of activities within a lesson.

Early Learning Goal: Personal, social and emotional development

During the Foundation Stage, pupils working towards the Early Learning Goals relating to personal, social and emotional development need to acquire a number of basic skills that will become increasingly important as they develop. These include:

- independence in carrying out activities
- attention, concentration and sitting quietly
- independence within the environment
- independent use of resources.

(DfEE/QCA 2000a: 28–43)

Pupils with ASD may have difficulties with these areas of learning and may have individual targets to work towards achieving them. The work system is one strategy within the Structured Teaching approach that may help pupils to become more organised and independent in their learning.

CASE STUDY
Teaching a left to right work system with a 'finished' box

Sam is three years old and attends an integrated nursery. He is beginning to respond to his physical structure and transition object information and will now sit at a table when given a felt pen. Sam's organisational skills are poor and he has an individual target to complete some activities independently. He is being taught to work independently by completing one activity, provided on his worktable. When it is completed (with or without support at this stage) Sam is directed to put it into a large 'finished' box on his right (Figure 6.1). Sam has learnt, through direct one-to-one teaching, to complete some simple activities focusing on Early Learning Goals relating to language and literacy and mathematical development, and also activities to develop fine motor/eye–hand coordination.

Figure 6.1: Basic left to right work system with a 'finished' box: one task.

Sam is also encouraged to use a 'finished' box when completing other activities such as painting or playing in sand. This reinforces the concept of 'finished' for Sam and helps with making transitions to other activities.

Without a work system, Sam finds the completion of any task difficult; he quickly becomes anxious or overwhelmed by too many resources and frequently either leaves the area, or tips the activity onto the floor. Sam's teacher is responding to Sam's individual learning needs by providing him with an organisational system and routine. Sam is learning to be independent in carrying out activities and is being encouraged to develop attention, concentration and 'quiet sitting' for a short period in order to complete a task. In addition, Sam is learning to become independent within the environment and to use resources independently. The introduction of a work system offers Sam's teacher and LSA a strategy for giving Sam time to practise the skills he has been taught while ensuring that the learning environment enables him to gain independence. As Sam progresses he will begin to use a left to right work system, taking his work from the shelf on the left, to complete a variety of tasks independently (Chapter 7).

Once a pupil has learnt to use a basic left to right work system with a 'finished' box independently, the system can be extended depending on the pupil's attention and concentration span. Pupils may begin by completing one task before moving on to the next activity; for example Sam may sort big and little items, place the finished work into his 'finished' box, then play in the sand. Pupils who can concentrate for longer periods may be asked to complete two, three or more tasks before moving on to the next activity. Another way of developing the system is to teach pupils to stack their finished work on a shelf on their right, rather than put it into a 'finished' box.

Organisation and study skills, developing personal autonomy and making choices

Curriculum guidance for teaching pupils with learning difficulties identifies the need for pupils to develop organisation and study skills in all subjects, and in all key stages. Examples include 'completing a task' and 'taking responsibility for tasks' by working independently (QCA 2001b: 15). In addition, the guidance for PSHE and citizenship indicates the need to develop personal autonomy and control across the curriculum (QCA 2001f: 9). For example, in Key Stage 3, pupils should be provided with opportunities for making choices, for example relating to break time activities. The use of a work system can help pupils to develop organisation and study skills, increase independence and control and offer opportunities for making choices. The following example illustrates these aspects.

CASE STUDY
Left to right work system

Martin is 14 and is in Year 9 attending a special school for pupils with severe learning difficulties. He is placed in a specialist class for six pupils with autism. Martin spends much of his time in his base room but also goes to other classrooms for some lessons. Martin understands the physical environment through the use of physical structure and he uses an object schedule independently. He is able to use a left to right work system in the classroom to complete up to four tasks during a lesson. Martin takes one task at a time from a table on his left and puts the completed task in a filing tray (or a 'finished' box, depending on the task) on his right (Figure 6.2). Two objects are placed in transparent bags on the wall in front of Martin. These objects indicate what he can do when he has finished all tasks. When he has finished his work, Martin chooses his next activity by taking one of the objects; for example he may choose between using a personal stereo in the leisure area of the classroom or using a computer.

Figure 6.2: Left to right work system: multiple tasks.

Martin uses his work system for independent working during literacy and numeracy lessons. He also uses his independent work system to consolidate skills that he has recently learnt in a variety of curriculum areas.

As Martin is required to work in other areas of the school, he uses a similar work system to help him with organisation. Martin is also able to use this system when working alongside peers in class lessons. For example, he has been taught to 'sort' utensils and rubbish into appropriate containers during one-to-one teaching sessions. Consequently during food technology lessons, Martin uses a left to right system: his utensils and ingredients are placed in containers on his left and items that are finished with are put into containers on his right (washing-up bowl for utensils, bin for rubbish). As in his main classroom, objects are used to indicate to Martin what happens when the lesson is finished: sometimes this is a choice of two activities, sometimes one object is provided to indicate what's next when there is no choice. The same system is used during art and design and science lessons. Without this organisational work system, Martin would become disorganised and a disproportionate amount of staff time would then be taken up with getting him organised. The use of the work system means that Martin can organise himself more independently during lessons and can consequently focus on the lesson content, rather than trying to organise his materials. He can complete tasks independently and is empowered to make choices, thus developing personal autonomy.

Martin uses his system by taking work from his left in any order. Some pupils will be able to match colours, shapes, pictures, letters or numbers and following their system enables them to complete activities in the order that the teacher requires (see Ricky's case study considered next). This allows for the teacher to plan for a sequence of tasks within a lesson or activity.

Organisation and study skills, managing behaviour and developing communication

Work systems are used to help pupils to develop organisation and study skills and to help pupils to concentrate and to complete a range of tasks set by the teacher. The work system can be used for independent work, but also during group lessons and for play. Pupils who can follow sequences of visual cues to complete several different tasks can develop their organisational skills in a number of ways. The work system can be utilised to increase a pupil's attention, interest and motivation, help him to manage independent work time and to complete tasks independently. This may lead to an increased ability to manage his own behaviour, often a priority area as challenging behaviour may present 'potential barriers to learning' that teachers need to overcome. In addition, the work system can be used to help pupils to generalise their learning into different contexts and can provide opportunities for developing spontaneous communication. The example below illustrates a work system that requires the pupil to follow a sequence of tasks in a given order and to use the work system in different learning contexts.

CASE STUDY
Left to right colour matching work system

Ricky is six years old, has ASD and learning difficulties and attends specialist autism provision within a school for children with a range of special educational needs. He attends the specialist class for the majority of his time, but integrates into a Year 1 class twice each week for social activities and structured play. Without structure Ricky is disorganised and becomes anxious when trying to find resources, knowing how much work to do and what to do with work he has finished, resulting in aimless wandering and flitting between activities without completing tasks. Ricky uses a photo schedule (Chapter 5) and is able to match colours and shapes. He has been taught to use a colour/shape matching work system (Figure 6.3) within his independent work area and is able to stay on task and to complete up to four tasks during a session.

Ricky's work is set up on a shelf on his left, each task labelled with a coloured pocket. Ricky follows a top to bottom list of corresponding colour/shape cards, placed on a Velcro strip on his desk, by taking the top card, matching it to the corresponding work task and completing that task. He completes all tasks in this way by working his way down his list of colour cards. Completed work is put onto a shelf to his right. Ricky can check his progress and knows when he has finished his work as the colour/shape cards have all gone from his desk. Ricky also knows what to do when his work is finished. Pinned to the wall are two photographs of activities that Ricky may choose from when he has finished his work. When he has completed all tasks, Ricky makes his choice and takes the appropriate photograph to an adult to request his chosen activity; thus his work system incorporates a meaningful opportunity to develop the key skill of communication.

Ricky uses his work system for independent working during literacy, numeracy and other lessons. This organisational system reduces Ricky's wandering behaviour and helps him to concentrate and to complete tasks. His attention span has increased and he has moved from completing one task to completing four. He is motivated to complete the work for several reasons: he understands the system and routine, he sees he is making progress, and he knows when he is finished and what he will do next. This gives Ricky some control and personal autonomy over what happens to him and increases his self-esteem and independence. Ricky is now beginning to use the work system in other learning contexts, including structured play and group activities.

Structured play

Ricky uses a similar colour/shape matching system for structured play activities in the play area. Without the system, Ricky is less likely to direct his attention to the play materials and more likely to flit around the area. By using the colour/shape matching system with a clear finish, Ricky is enabled to use a wide range of play materials and to complete the activities with support. The system is set up at a structured play table placed at the edge of the play area. Ricky knows

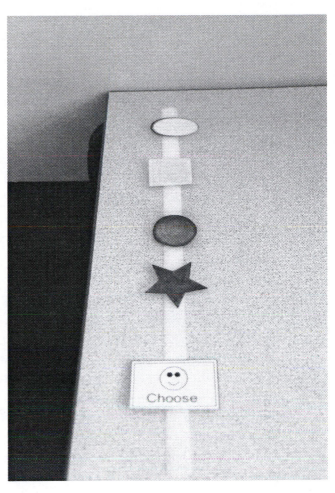

Figure 6.3: Colour matching work system.

what will happen when the play session is finished as a photo is placed on the wall indicating 'what's next'. Ricky's teacher is now developing this to encourage Ricky to play in closer proximity to peers. Ricky uses the work system to find the play activity. He then plays independently, but in proximity to another pupil, with the play materials and places them in a 'finished' container on the right. Later he may use play cooperatively with another peer, still using a work system to help him to be organised. The same system is used when Ricky integrates into the Year 1 class where he is learning to play alongside peers within a defined physical area.

Play is not limited to structured sessions, and opportunities are provided to encourage Ricky to develop interactive play. However, the work system is a useful strategy to help Ricky improve his ability to attend, concentrate and to complete play activities with peers, rather than to wander aimlessly. The same system can be used for outside play where activities are set up in discrete areas. For example, each activity is colour coded and individuals can follow a colour matching work system to move from one activity to another. In this way, pupils can be directed to specific activities, but can also make choices as part of the work system. For example, a pupil may be directed to the red area for bikes, followed by ball games in the green area, followed by a choice. If the pupil likes to wander, this can be included in the choices on offer. Playtimes can then be utilised to teach pupils how to use play resources, and also to have some free time during which choices can be made. If pupils are taught to make their choice, then communicate their choice to an adult, the system thus provides excellent opportunities to communicate. It is important here to distinguish between the schedule and the work system: the schedule tells a pupil it is playtime, the work system (at any level) then helps the pupil organise his time during playtime.

Emphasising 'finished' to manage behaviour

The National Curriculum and the QCA guidance for teaching pupils with learning difficulties identify the need for pupils to develop strategies for managing their own behaviour (DfEE/QCA 1999a, b; QCA 2001a). Sometimes behaviours occur due to poor organisational skills and confusion. For example, prior to introducing a work system, Ricky would often throw materials when he had finished with them. The use of a 'finished' container on a shelf or table to his right has reduced this behaviour significantly in the classroom. Hence, Ricky uses a 'finished' container at lunchtimes to prevent him from throwing cutlery and food. A washing-up bowl is placed on a table on his right for Ricky to put all items that he is finished with. Ricky's teacher intends to teach Ricky to take this bowl to the kitchen when lunchtime is finished. The same approach is used in lessons such as art and design, to prevent materials from being thrown.

Ricky has been able to utilise a work system in a number of ways. He is developing a number of key skills and skills relating to PSHE as indicated in the QCA guidance (QCA 2001b, f). In particular, he is increasing his capacity to concentrate and complete tasks within different curriculum areas and he is learning to manage his own behaviour more successfully. As he becomes more confident in using the work system, he can approach new activities provided within the same structure, thus beginning to generalise what he has learnt. Ricky's structure now helps to clarify the purpose of different areas of the classroom, reduces distractions, lets him know what will be happening through the use of his schedule and helps him to complete work by providing a work system. Further visual information will then help Ricky to understand what he is to do, and how to do it (Chapter 7).

Increasing independence, working alongside others and communication

Work systems are used to enable pupils to work independently in a variety of contexts. Some pupils need to practise independent organisation skills within discrete work areas, away from other pupils. However, work systems can also be used to encourage pupils to develop their ability to work with others, as this is a key skill required in all curriculum areas. Equally the work system provides an effective strategy for increasing independence and developing communication. Many pupils with ASD need to be encouraged to develop their spontaneous communication within naturally occurring contexts. Frequently, pupils do not ask for help, tell the teacher when they have finished or ask for information. Once a pupil is familiar with the work system, opportunities can be provided to encourage him to communicate spontaneously.

CASE STUDY
Number matching work system requiring movement around the classroom

Leila attends specialist provision for pupils with special educational needs, two of whom have ASD. This provision is part of a mainstream primary school. Leila is nine years old and has autism and learning difficulties. Leila has poor short-term memory and attention span and cannot recall the sequences of activities that take place during the day. Similarly, Leila cannot remember the sequence of tasks she is to complete, for example within a science lesson. She becomes anxious when she does not know what to do and gets very upset when she cannot find resources required for a lesson. In addition, Leila is reluctant to communicate with adults, particularly those who are unfamiliar to her.

Leila has learnt to use a work system that helps her to complete sequences of tasks independently. Leila's work tasks are numbered and she follows a top to bottom number list on her desk to complete tasks in sequence. Like Ricky, she takes the top card and matches it to the corresponding numbered task. However, Leila is being encouraged to work alongside peers and to become increasingly independent, so her work is not set up in a left to right system. Instead, Leila fetches work from a shelf within the work area and returns it when it is completed. This storage space is also used by other pupils, so Leila needs to ensure that she takes the correct work for her and also has to cooperate with other children who are fetching and returning work (Figure 6.4). Leila knows what to do when her work is finished as a symbol for the next lesson, or 'choose', is placed at the bottom of her number list (this directs her to a class choice board).

The structure provided for Leila encourages her to work alongside peers, in relation to both her physical structure and her work system. She is increasing her independence and is less

Figure 6.4: Number work system, matching to labelled work – shared working area.

anxious about getting organised and remembering what tasks she is to do. The work system provides her with visual cues that help her to complete tasks in the sequence required. Without the system she cannot remember the instructions and becomes upset when she has not completed tasks in the correct order.

Leila's work system also provides opportunities for her to communicate with adults. For example, Leila is reluctant to ask for help and will sometimes sit and cry or take her work that is not finished back to the shelf. Asking for help is one of Leila's individual targets relating to PSHE and citizenship and the work system is one strategy used to provide her with opportunities to do so (DfEE/QCA 1999a: 138). Leila's LSA has placed a reminder on Leila's desk and is teaching her to take the symbol for 'help' to an adult (Figure 6.5).

Figure 6.5: Help card reminder used within the work system.

While the majority of Leila's tasks can be completed independently, the teacher has begun to provide opportunities to encourage Leila to seek help from an adult. For example, some of the resources needed to complete a task are missing from the work tray or folder, thus Leila needs to ask for help to find the resources. In this case a similar reminder to ask for help is placed with the task. Reminders can be provided to encourage pupils to communicate for other reasons, for example to tell the teacher when they are finished. Visual reminders within tasks may also indicate what materials the pupil needs to go and find, encouraging greater independence.

Integrating in a mainstream class

Leila's work system is providing her with necessary organisational skills, and with increasing independence. Leila is beginning to work alongside others and to cooperate with them within a shared space. The same work system is used in the mainstream classroom where Leila works independently at a table adjacent to another pupil. A storage area has been allocated for Leila, but also for other pupils to use when they are using the 'office' workstation. Other pupils with special educational needs in the class, for example a pupil with attention deficit and hyperactivity disorder, have benefited from the use of the work system approach.

When Leila joins the mainstream class for music lessons, a similar work system approach is used to help Leila to get organised within the lesson. Leila's LSA prepares the system prior to the lesson in collaboration with the music teacher, using numbered symbols to indicate the order of activities such as listening to music, singing and playing instruments. This organisational system means that Leila's LSA can concentrate on supporting Leila with the lesson content and concepts, rather than spending most of the time helping Leila to get organised. While Leila is not expected to complete all of the music-related work independently, she can still use the work system to organise herself.

As Leila develops key skills relating to organisation, communication and working with others, additional visual information is used to extend these skills and to help Leila to begin to develop early thinking and problem-solving skills (Chapter 7).

Work systems in different learning contexts: PSHE and citizenship

Work systems are often introduced within one learning context, such as the pupil's main classroom or learning support base. However, the work system can be used within a widening range of contexts as the pupil increases in independence and confidence. As pupils are required to move from lesson to lesson, portable work systems can be set up to facilitate organisation, independence and personal autonomy. In PSHE and citizenship, pupils should be learning, for example, to develop confidence and responsibility, to make real choices, to ask for help and to share equipment (DfEE/QCA 1999a: 137–8). Guidance for teaching pupils with learning difficulties also indicates key learning areas in PSHE and citizenship, including taking responsibility, feeling positive, developing personal autonomy and making choices (QCA 2001f). The work system can play a role in helping pupils to develop their abilities in these areas that are of particular significance for pupils with ASD. The following example illustrates how a work system helps a pupil to increase his independence by taking responsibility for organising his work within the structure of a work system, to make choices and simple decisions, to share equipment and to increase his self-esteem.

CASE STUDY
Portable number/letter lists, sharing resources

David attends a specialist school for pupils with ASD. He is 11 years old and has Asperger Syndrome. He is preparing for transition to secondary provision with the support of a LSA. David follows his symbol/word schedule independently and takes a portable version with him to the secondary school. David's work is kept on a shelf and in his drawer and tasks are numbered or lettered. He uses a number/letter work system in his main classroom, which consists of a list of numbers and letters written onto a note pad. David uses his list to complete tasks in sequence, crossing out each task as it is completed (Figure 6.6). At the bottom of the list he has an instruction to tell the teacher or LSA when he is finished. They can then check his work with him.

A symbol/written card on his desk also reminds David where to put work that is not finished. This is particularly important if pupils are not expected to complete the work in

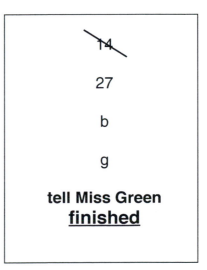

Figure 6.6: Number/letter list to cross off.

75

one session. Some pupils will find this confusing and get upset; in this case a clear place for 'unfinished' work will be as important as the 'finished' place.

The work system is helping David to increasingly take responsibility for organising himself and increasing his personal autonomy. In addition, David is no longer provided with all necessary materials to complete a task. He is provided with a symbol/word reminder within a task that requires him to find the resources that he needs, thus providing the opportunity to make simple decisions relating to his everyday life.

Resources are kept centrally so that all pupils may access them when needed. Sometimes David cannot find the resources he needs as other pupils have them. A symbol/word reminder placed near to the resources table reminds David to find who has the resource and ask if he can share. Thus David is being provided with opportunities to work towards sharing equipment with his peers (PSHE and citizenship 5f, DfEE/QCA 1999a: 138). Note that in this curriculum area David is working within an earlier key stage in order for him to be provided with 'suitable learning challenges'.

Integration and transition from primary to secondary provision

When David integrates into a local mainstream primary school for mathematics, and when he visits his new secondary provision, he takes a portable schedule in a ring binder. The ring binder is then also used for his work system. David's folder contains his daily schedule at the front and a note pad for his work system for each lesson. His number/letter list to identify tasks within a lesson is sometimes prepared in advance by the LSA, in collaboration with the teachers, or can be written during the lesson by the LSA.

David follows the list to complete set tasks and to ask for his work to be checked. Clearly this requires preparation and collaboration between David's LSA and his teachers. Sometimes information is not available until the lesson, or requirements change. The LSA can produce, add to or amend David's list during the lesson if required. In addition, the teacher sometimes offers a choice in relation to the order in which tasks should be completed and in this case David's list will indicate where there is a choice (Figure 6.7). This provides opportunities for David to make simple decisions and to solve simple everyday problems (QCA 2001b: 9). For example, he may choose a particular task because the resources he needs for the other task are being used. He can then negotiate to use them after the other pupil has finished with them. In the meantime he can get on with another task.

David is using a work system strategy for independent work, but also within lessons when he might need support. As with Leila, a LSA then spends time more productively supporting David with lesson concepts when required. Thus he can still find the work for himself, he knows in what order to complete it and he knows what to do when it is finished. He is moving independently to a number of places to find and return work and he is beginning to share resources. David is taking responsibility for himself, making choices and developing independence. His work system is not dissimilar to the lists many of us set up for ourselves when faced with a large number of tasks to complete.

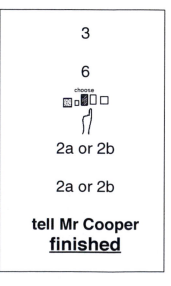

Figure 6.7: Number/letter list with choice of order of tasks.

Work systems in inclusive settings: working with others

Work systems can be useful in inclusive classrooms and may provide one 'reasonable step' to help a pupil to be included (DfES 2001a). Some pupils with ASD will find the organisational requirements in a mainstream classroom stressful and overwhelming. This may lead to inappropriate behaviours such as work refusal or avoidance, aggression or excessive anxiety that may threaten their ability to be included. LSAs may find themselves spending considerable time supporting the pupil in relation to his organisational difficulties and valuable time is lost for concentrating on learning lesson concepts. The use of a work system may help the pupil to overcome difficulties with organisation, possibly reducing or removing a potential barrier to learning. The work system provides one strategy for enabling pupils to be included by empowering individuals to organise themselves. The work system can be used to facilitate independent working and can also be used within lessons where a pupil may need support. In addition, while work systems are often effective in facilitating individual working, they can also be used to develop pupils' abilities to work with others. The following example is illustrative of a work system that is flexible and used in a variety of contexts for independent and cooperative work.

CASE STUDY
Written work system, combined with schedule

Sarah is nine-years-old and has a diagnosis of ASD. She attends her local primary school and is supported in Year 4 by a LSA for 75 per cent of lessons. Sarah has good expressive language, although this can mask her difficulties with comprehension. She has poor organisational and sequencing abilities and is unable to recall sequences of instructions. Sarah uses a written, daily schedule (Chapter 5) and is also helped with additional symbols when needed, for example at times of anxiety.

Sarah uses a work system that combines number and written instructions. Her work system is contained in a filing box, divided into lessons (Figure 6.8). Sarah finds the appropriate file card for the lesson and checks off each task as it is completed. Sarah knows 'what's next' from a written statement at the end of her final task. Sarah's work system indicates what work she is to do and in what order to complete the tasks.

The LSA usually prepares the work system for specific lessons, including literacy and numeracy, after consulting the teacher to find out what Sarah is to do. The LSA is given time to prepare Sarah's work system for the following day's lessons during the final part of the afternoon. The LSA has prepared a variety of numbered and written cards that are laminated and can be reused. In addition, a number of cards are blank so that the LSA can indicate new tasks during a lesson. Sarah is being encouraged to listen to the teacher's verbal instructions and to write them onto her work system for herself; this is helped by teachers who write instructions for the class on the whiteboard.

Sarah knows what work to do, how much she has to do and what happens when she has finished. She is able to cope with alterations to her work system and will amend instructions

Figure 6.8: Work system in filing box.

herself when directed. Also she is learning to cope when, for example, there is no time to complete a task and will cross it off from her list when asked to.

Sarah's work system enables her to be independent in relation to organisation. Without the system, Sarah would become confused and distressed and would often be taken out of the lesson by the LSA to calm down. Consequently she would miss some of the lesson and this would add to her distress. Sarah's number/written work system is quick and easy to produce, yet is empowering for Sarah in relation to developing independence and helping her to be included.

Using work systems in cooperative activities

Sarah uses her work system for most lessons. This enables her to be organised in a range of subject areas. In addition to using her system for independent working, she also refers to it when working with a small group. This has been developed to encourage Sarah to cooperate with other pupils in group tasks. For example, Sarah's class prepared a report for a school newsletter about their recent sports day, focusing on writing, speaking and listening and ICT (English Key Stage 2: Writing PoS 1a, 1e, 2e: 56; Speaking and listening 3a, 3b: 50; ICT Key Stage 2 PoS 1a, 1b, 2a, 3b, 4b: 100–1; DfEE/QCA 1999a). A 'jigsaw' approach was used to divide several tasks between groups (Rose 1991). Tasks included:

- interviewing pupils to identify quotes and sub-headings for the report;
- writing the report;
- sorting, selecting and preparing photographs taken with a digital camera during the event in order to prepare a photograph collage, with captions.

All pupils worked together on editing and preparing the final report. Sarah's individual objectives were to make choices of pictures, to discuss reasons for her choices with two other pupils, to write captions and to share and take turns in discussing photographs. Sarah's work system indicates her tasks but also reminds her of her peers' tasks (Figure 6.9). Additional written instructions were provided for Sarah in order for her to use the software appropriately (Chapter 7).

Each group reported to the class on what they had done, and why they had done it that way. Sarah's work system card helped her to recall what her group had done and to tell the class, thus offering an opportunity for her to reflect upon and evaluate the group's activity as part of their work on key skills (DfEE/QCA 1999a).

Sarah's work system enables her to cooperate with her peers and be successful in completing her part of the task. The combination of a work system within a jigsaw approach is sometimes a useful strategy for helping pupils with ASD to be included in group tasks. Pupils can be allocated a part of the task that is most likely to interest them or that uses their strengths and the work system is used to help with understanding what they have to do, how much and what to do when finished. While Sarah can work alongside her peers, some pupils are not yet able to do so. Nevertheless they may be included in the lesson by being allocated a part of the task and completing it at their

**English and ICT
Preparing a newsletter report**

1. Whole class: listen ☐

2. Group 1
   • select photos ☐
   • Jane choose 2 (Sarah listen) ☐
   • Sarah choose 2 tell others why you have chosen ☐
   • Jack choose 2 (Sarah listen) ☐

3. Organise layout together ☐

4. Write captions ☐

5. Whole class edit report Sarah listen then tell class what the group has done ☐

6. Check your schedule ☐

Figure 6.9: Work system in a group activity.

independent workstation, using their work system. They can then make their contribution to the final piece of work.

Sarah is using her work system to complete activities independently and to work with others. The final example illustrates how this can be extended within a secondary school setting and lead to the transition to adult life and the world of work.

Using work systems in secondary mainstream settings and work-related learning

Work systems are flexible and should be designed to meet individual learning needs. For pupils included in mainstream secondary schools, the work system can be a helpful strategy both for classroom-based learning and also for learning within the community, for example during work experience. Work systems that are part of a schedule may be helpful to some pupils and may be used within personal organisers or folders. These can be adapted to be used in a wide range of contexts. The use of a work system is not confined to individuals with ASD; indeed many of us use work systems in our everyday lives by writing lists and crossing off completed tasks, often with great satisfaction! The difference is that most of us can set up and implement our own, while people with ASD need help with each part of the process. The use of the work system is one strategy that can help prepare pupils with ASD for life beyond school, within college and workplace contexts. The National Curriculum indicates that pupils in Key Stages 3 and 4 should be engaged in 'learning for work' by continuing to develop key skills through opportunities for 'work-related learning' (DfEE/QCA 1999b: 24–5). Many pupils with ASD will require structured approaches to enable them to participate in work-related learning and to learn how to organise themselves in the workplace. The following example illustrates the use of a work system in school and during work experience.

CASE STUDY
Written work systems preparing for adult life

Adam is 15 years old and has Asperger Syndrome. He attends a local mainstream secondary school and is studying for his GCSEs. Adam uses a student planner that incorporates a written daily schedule (Chapter 5). The schedule also includes his work system combining a written and number system (Figure 6.10). Adam prepares this with a LSA each morning at the learning support base.

Monday   **Week A**

8.30a.m.   Learning support: check schedule for the day

8.45a.m.   English 101 (LSA: Mrs Smith) **(English wallet)**
Poetry composition
listen
write poem
show Mr Wall

10.30a.m.   Break: library or outside

11.00a.m.   Maths 205 (LSA: Mrs Taylor) **(maths wallet)**
Fractions
listen
worksheet 3
homework – worksheet 4

11.45a.m.   Learning support – independent study time   **3a   6b   2a   break**

12.15p.m.   Lunch break: outside or learning support

1.30p.m.   PE: field (what equipment?)

3.00p.m.   Learning support: check homework diary and schedule for tomorrow

Reminders:

raise my hand rather than interrupt

work that is not finished can be filed as unfinished – check with the tutor when to finish it

---

Figure 6.10: Work system incorporated on schedule.

Adam uses his work system for independent work and for parts of lessons in the mainstream school. He has daily opportunities for working independently within the learning support base to consolidate learnt skills and to develop his concentration and attention span for lengthier periods. During these work sessions, Adam uses a series of labelled 'in' and 'out' office trays that contain labelled tasks, corresponding to the tasks indicated on his schedule for that particular lesson. During lessons in mainstream classrooms, Adam has learnt to construct his work system by writing the teacher's verbal instructions onto his schedule in the appropriate place. In addition, he has labelled plastic zip wallets in his file to keep additional instructions that have been prepared by learning support staff and equipment for particular lessons (Chapter 7). His work system reminds him when he needs to use these items. Adam's work system sometimes incorporates questions to remind him to check he has everything he needs.

Adam also uses a work system to organise his homework; this is prepared with his teacher or LSA in the learning support department. He uses his work system to overcome organisational difficulties and to ensure that he has essential resources for lessons. It also helps him to complete homework and to know who to hand it in to and when.

Work experience

The work system was used when Adam went to a local library for work experience. Adam's schedule was prepared with support from a mentor identified in the workplace. Each morning, Adam's work system was incorporated onto his schedule with help from the mentor (Figure 6.11). This enabled Adam to know what jobs he had to complete, in what order and when breaks would occur. Further visual instructions were available to help him to complete each job and to structure his break times (Chapter 7).

Thursday 17th May

8.30a.m.	Library
	Job: stock replacement (tell Miss Thorpe when finished)
10.15a.m.	Break **Make coffee read magazine**
10.45a.m.	**Job: returns desk**
12.00 noon	Lunch break
1.00p.m.	**Job: photocopying (tell Mrs Green when finished)**
2.45p.m.	Break
3.00p.m.	**Job: tidy store (tell Miss Thorpe when finished)**
4.00p.m.	Home

Reminder:

when I need help, ask Miss Thorpe

Figure 6.11: Work system on schedule used for work experience.

By the end of the work experience, Adam was able to complete all allocated jobs independently and was described as a conscientious and reliable worker.

Adam's combined schedule and work system is used to help him to become as independent as possible, both in school and in other settings. In addition, Adam is provided with opportunities for making choices and decisions, within both the schedule and the work system. The structure that Adam has learnt to use is transferable to contexts outside school and will be useful for him in adulthood.

Conclusion

Work systems are an essential part of Structured Teaching that enable pupils to become organised, to concentrate, stay engaged and to complete tasks set. They can be an effective strategy for responding to the particular learning styles of individuals with ASD by providing clear visual cues and organisation. Within a work system, pupils who are ready can be provided with opportunities for communication and making choices and decisions. Work systems are individualised to help to improve curriculum access and facilitate inclusion in different curriculum areas (Table 6.1).

Table 6.1: Access to the curriculum through use of work systems.

Curriculum area	Work systems promote
Early Learning Goals: Personal, social and emotional development	• Independence in carrying out activities • Independence in the environment • Independent use of resources • Concentration and sitting quietly
National Curriculum: Key skills	• Communication • Working with others
Planning, teaching and assessing the curriculum for pupils with learning difficulties: Developing skills	• Organisation and study skills • Problem solving
PSHE and citizenship	• Managing own behaviour • Self-control • Personal autonomy • Making choices • Taking responsibility • Feeling positive
Other aspects of the school curriculum	• Work-related learning

As with the other elements of structure, assessment of developmental and cognitive abilities will be critical in establishing which type of work system will be helpful for an individual pupil. The aim for the pupil is to provide a system that is most functional and leads to greatest independence for him. This will require individual target setting and careful monitoring and reviewing to ensure that the work system is effective. An individualised work system provides a structured organisational framework that should enable pupils to participate.

Schedules and work systems are helpful in that they provide pupils with important information, in a form that they best understand, about the sequence of events during the day and about how to get organised. If the schedule and work system are appropriate to the individual needs of the pupil, he will know what is going to happen, when and where. He will also know how much work he has to do, where to get it from, how he is progressing, what to do with the work when he has finished and what he should do next. This does not however complete the picture. The pupil may understand from his schedule that it is time for the numeracy lesson and he may find the work he has to do; however, when he looks at the task he may be unsure as to how to complete it. Additional visual information is needed so pupils know how to complete an activity or task. Chapter 7 provides examples that illustrate how additional visual information helps pupils with understanding and completing a variety of tasks.

7 Visual information: adding meaning

Overview

Visual structure can be used to organise, clarify and differentiate tasks and assignments. It provides the pupil with information about how to complete a task and how to use the required materials. Because visual skills are often especially strong in autism, and generally stronger than pupils' receptive language skills, visual information can be very helpful in developing understanding and helping pupils to carry out class assignments. If pupils are taught to look for visual information in all of their activities, they can use this information to understand and perform their work more effectively. Three kinds of visual information are used extensively: visual clarity, visual organisation and visual instructions.

Visual clarity draws or engages the pupil's attention to important or relevant information. It is a way of explaining and directing the person with autism to the aspects of the task that are most central. Colour coding and highlighting are the two most common ways of utilising visual clarity.

Visual organisation involves the way that space and containers are used to organise tasks or assignments. The organisation can convey a sense of orderliness that is very helpful for people with ASD. The organisation of a task can also limit the focus of their attention and make it easier for them to identify and stay attentive to the most relevant information. Organising containers, limiting materials and dividing and stabilising tasks are effective ways to utilise visual organisation. These organisational strategies allow pupils to focus on their tasks instead of endlessly, and usually unsuccessfully, organising their materials.

Visual instructions are written or pictorial cues that give pupils information about how to do an assignment or put the distinct parts of a task together correctly. They can include written instructions, pictured instructions with single words, pictured instructions, jigs, or product samples (actual prototypes of what you want the child to make). Pupils who consistently use visual instructions are much more flexible because the instructions can always be changed when the task demands need to be altered. The rigidity that sometimes characterises pupils with autism is reduced when they become engaged in following such instructions, rather than always doing tasks in their own idiosyncratic way. The basis for this greater flexibility, for pupils and teachers, is because instructions can be varied depending upon the approach or outcome required. The pupil is learning to follow the instructions as the routine and these instructions can be altered to increase flexibility and to encourage simple problem solving.

Using additional visual information as a strategy for differentiation

The principles for inclusion in the National Curriculum identify the need for teachers to set suitable learning challenges, to respond to learning needs and to overcome potential barriers to learning (DfEE/QCA 1999a: 30–7, 1999b: 32–9). The predominantly visual learning style of many pupils with ASD means that in order to address these principles it will be essential to provide additional visual information that will add meaning to specific tasks and activities. Useful examples are provided within the inclusion statement that illustrate how teachers can address these principles including for example 'using teaching approaches appropriate to different learning styles' (DfEE/QCA 1999a: 32); 'using visual and written materials in different formats, including print, symbol, text . . .'; 'using alternative and augmentative communication, including signs and symbols' (34) and 'using ICT, visual and other materials to increase pupils' knowledge of the wider world' (34). The use of visual information provides a useful strategy for increasing pupils' understanding of specific tasks and activities and can be an effective way of differentiating tasks for pupils with ASD.

Improving the physical structure and introducing schedules and work systems are helpful elements of Structured Teaching that enable pupils to make more sense of what is expected of them. These strategies can help pupils to concentrate, to understand what will be happening and to develop independent organisational skills. In addition, pupils will need further visual information to increase their understanding of a lesson and what they need to do in order to complete tasks. For example, the schedule tells the pupil it is time for numeracy, a work system is used to enable the pupil to organise his work and additional visual information increases the pupil's understanding of the task itself. Elements of visual information can help to add meaning to tasks and activities, both subject based and in relation to other aspects of the curriculum, for example assemblies and playtimes. The purpose of this chapter is to provide examples that illustrate how the use of visual information can enhance meaning in a range of lessons and activities. Differentiation of tasks using visual information is individualised according to cognitive and developmental abilities, hence the examples provided may not be automatically transferable to other pupils. Examples are provided to illustrate the principles of using the additional visual information that teachers and LSAs will need in order to adapt and differentiate tasks, based on an assessment of each pupil's individual learning needs. Pupils will need to be taught to look for visual information to help them to understand concepts presented during a lesson, what is required to complete tasks and how to begin to problem solve.

Visual information can be used to add meaning to tasks and activities in a number of different contexts:

- independent practising and consolidating skills that have previously been taught
- independent work times, for example during the literacy hour
- increasing meaning of tasks within group and whole-class lessons
- developing problem-solving and investigative skills
- developing independence in everyday routines
- developing understanding of other activities such as assembly and playtime.

Visual information is a useful strategy for differentiating planning in all subjects and can also be used to help pupils to develop key skills and thinking skills. The following examples illustrate ways in which visual information can be used to differentiate for pupils with ASD. As teachers plan from a range of resources, examples are cross-referenced to the Early Learning Goals' stepping stones, National Curriculum programmes of study, the literacy and numeracy frameworks, DfEE/QCA schemes of work and QCA guidance on planning, teaching and assessing the curriculum for pupils with learning difficulties.

Introducing additional visual information

The elements of visual structure for differentiating tasks include the need to consider visual clarity, visual organisation of tasks and visual instructions. For pupils in the early years and for pupils with severe learning difficulties, tasks can be visually structured to ensure that the concept or purpose of the task is clarified. Visual organisation of the task materials can also help to increase understanding of what is required. For many pupils with ASD the organisation of task materials will be important. Just as pupils may have difficulties with organising themselves in relation to where to get their work from and where to put it when it is finished, equally they have difficulties with organising the materials within a task. The work system helps the pupil to find his work and to put it away when it is finished. Additional visual information is then required to help him to organise the task materials. Sometimes pupils will not complete tasks due to confusion or anxiety relating to the materials. For example, items for sorting that fall onto the floor may cause distress and the pupil may not complete the task. Organisation of materials into containers that are fixed may alleviate this anxiety and enable the pupil to complete the task. At this level, additional visual instructions are not used; the task is visually clarified and organised to ensure that the pupil will not require any further instructions.

CASE STUDY
Introducing structured tasks

Sam is three years old and attends an integrated nursery. He is learning to use transition objects to move between activities in the nursery and is being taught how to use a basic work system with a 'finished' box to develop organisational skills. Sam is frequently overwhelmed when presented with too many materials and will often throw them onto the floor. During one-to-one teaching times, Sam is working towards Early Learning Goals in communication, language and literacy and mathematical development. He is presented with tasks that have been visually structured to clarify and enhance the meaning of what he is to do. Materials are organised into fixed containers so that he does not lose resources and each task is presented within a shoebox or tray to reduce the need for Sam to organise materials. Tasks are organised in a left to right or top to bottom sequence, hence all the materials are organised in containers on the left, or at the top, within the shoebox or tray. Sam is taught to follow left to right and top to bottom organisational routines as the first step to independence in completing tasks.

The following examples illustrate tasks that have been visually structured to help Sam to develop basic skills within the Foundation Curriculum. Resources have been chosen that are interesting and motivating to Sam.

Mathematical development

Sam is particularly interested in textures and shapes and is learning to match a range of materials through the use of visually structured tasks. He is currently working towards the Early Learning Goal: Mathematical Development/Stepping stone: 'show an interest in shape and space by playing with shapes or making arrangements with objects' (DfEE/QCA 2000a: 78). The following task is completed with adult support (Figure 7.1).

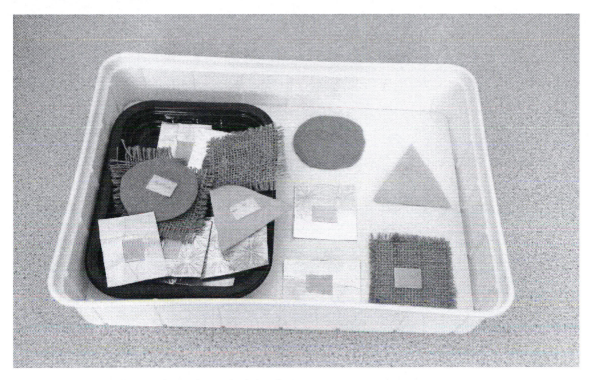

Figure 7.1: Independent task: mathematical development.

The shapes in this task are made of different fabrics as Sam likes to feel different textures so this interest helps him to make the correct match. Materials are organised left to right and Velcro is used to ensure the materials stay in place once matched. Sam does not have to organise any materials and can therefore concentrate on the task concepts. Similarly materials can be presented within a structured shoebox to help Sam to clearly see what he is supposed to do and to help reduce frustrations that may arise due to poor organisational skills. For example, later Sam will be taught to match and sort shapes without the texture cues (Figure 7.2). Introducing different shapes for Sam to sort varies this task and helps him to make progress. The visual organisation of the task helps Sam to focus on the sorting concept, rather than worry about organising himself.

Hand–eye coordination

Sam is also using play materials to work towards individual targets in relation to the Early Learning Goals, for example Communication, Language and Literacy/Stepping stone: 'engage in activities requiring hand–eye coordination' (DfEE/QCA 2000a: 66). The following example

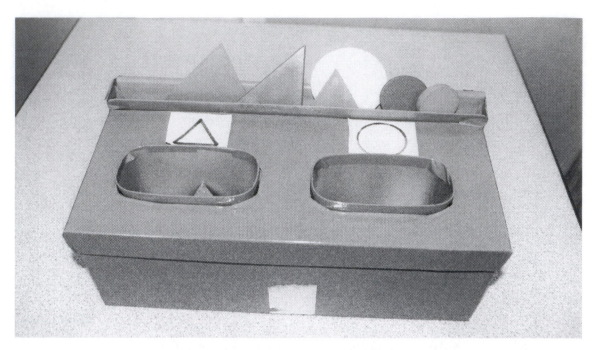

Figure 7.2: Developing independence: mathematical development.

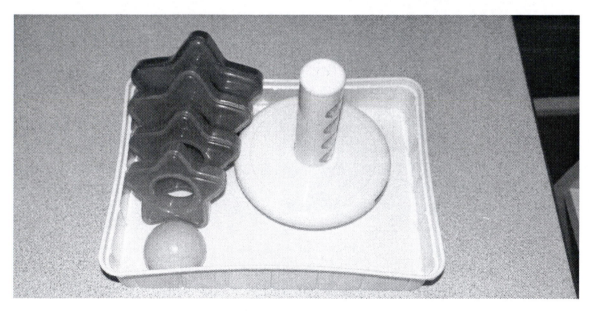

Figure 7.3: Independent task: hand–eye coordination.

illustrates how a stacking toy is organised to help Sam to practise hand–eye coordination (Figure 7.3). Again, this task has been organised for Sam to take the shapes from the left, working top to bottom, in order to complete stacking. Without the visual organisation of the resources, Sam would quickly become disorganised and confused as to what to do and would probably abandon the activity. Visual organisation enables Sam to understand how to complete activities; he still needs support at this stage but will become increasingly independent as he makes progress. Sam's activities and tasks are often visually structured by nursery assistants after working with the teacher during the planning stage. For example, the left to right and/or top to bottom organisation of materials can be used in a wide range of activities including cooking, water play and so on.

Sam is currently learning to complete activities with his LSA. Once he has learnt to complete a task he will be taught to practise his new skill during an independent work time, using his work system. This will provide Sam with opportunities to rehearse and consolidate new skills independently. As he learns new skills, these can be transferred to independent work time and he can continue to learn new skills within his one-to-one teaching times. Ongoing monitoring, recording and reviewing of Sam's independent tasks will be important to ensure that Sam continues to make progress and does not become bored by too much repetition. While he needs some repetition at this stage, in order to consolidate his learning, it is important to also consider progress within the independent work time. Sam's independent work tasks are curriculum referenced to the Early Learning Goals and linked to his IEP targets; this enables Sam's teacher to closely monitor Sam's progress and to update independent tasks when appropriate.

Visual information can be helpful to clarify the purpose of activities and tasks focusing on the Early Learning Goals. Older pupils with ASD and learning difficulties may also require this level of organisation and clarification to increase their understanding of what to do.

CASE STUDY
Developing structured tasks

Martin is 14 and is in Year 9 attending a special school for pupils with severe learning difficulties. He is placed in a specialist class for six pupils with autism. Martin uses an object schedule and a left to right work system. Additional visual information is used to help Martin to complete a variety of tasks independently. Martin has independent work times scheduled daily in order to provide opportunities for him to consolidate new skills and to practise independent organisational and study skills. These independent study times are used for subject-based tasks that are curriculum referenced and for working towards individual targets. Visual information is also used during group and class lessons, for example for tasks within a science lesson. In addition, Martin is helped by additional visual information to take part in other activities, for example mini-enterprise. Martin is helped to understand how to complete specific tasks by visual clarification and organisation. Martin's tasks are presented in varying containers including shoeboxes, trays, baskets and folders to increase his flexibility. The following examples illustrate how visual information is used to help Martin to work in small groups and independently and to improve communication.

Science

Visual information is used to help Martin complete tasks during class lessons. For example, in a series of science lessons pupils are observing reactions and mixtures (QCA/DfEE 2000 scheme of work for science Key Stage 3, unit 7f 'simple chemical reactions'). One of the lessons requires pupils to pour red cabbage water onto a variety of everyday substances to observe and record the outcomes. Martin is helped to record the results by grouping items that change to the same colour (pink or blue) and taking a photograph of each group. A structured task is prepared for Martin and a peer helps him to complete the task with some adult assistance. The visual information for this task is shown in Figure 7.4.

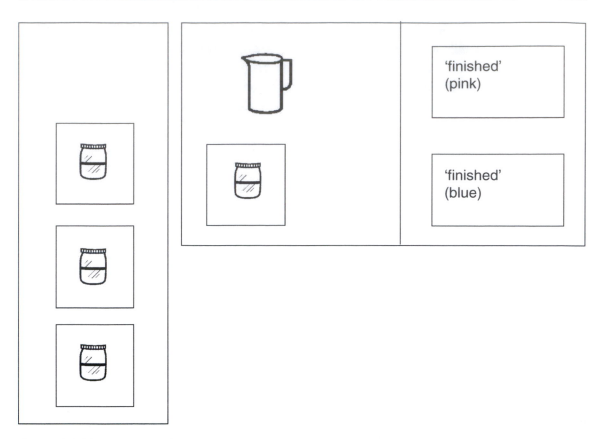

Figure 7.4: Visual organisation: science.

Martin and one peer follow the left to right organisation of the activity and materials to help them to test each item systematically. Coloured tape indicates how much cabbage water to pour into each container. The organisation of two 'finished' containers, coloured pink and blue, on the right also supports Martin and his peer to observe the reaction and colour and to make a decision as to where to place the mixture. Without this visual information, the pupils would become confused and this may lead to challenging behaviour. Visual information helps Martin to under-stand what he is to do and supports him in developing investigative skills. He still requires support from an adult during this lesson, but the LSA can now spend her time helping to reinforce the lesson concept, rather than organising the materials for the pupils. Through the use of visual structure, Martin is more likely to stay and participate in the lesson, achieving science P5 'they group objects and materials in terms of simple features or properties, for example . . . colour' and 'they engage in experimentation with a range of equipment in familiar and relevant situations' (QCA 2001e: 32).

Speaking and listening

As part of his work in English, Martin is being encouraged to communicate with his family about events at school and also to communicate with his teacher about events at home. In addition, he is further encouraged to communicate this information to staff at the respite centre which he attends one weekend per month. Martin has a diary that is used for this purpose. With the use of visual information, Martin completes the diary each day, with support, using objects, or logos from packaging, to represent what he has done, what he enjoyed and so on (Figure 7.5). This diary is one example of the ways in which Martin and other pupils are being provided with oppor-

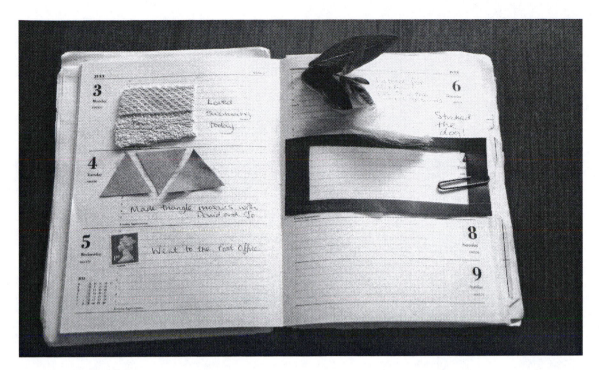

Figure 7.5: Visual clarity: communication.

tunities to 'be involved in making simple visual and/or tactile records which reflect their widening range of experiences' (QCA 2001c: 22).

This activity is supported by an adult, within a routine structure. The task is visually organised to follow a left to right organisation of resources. Objects and logos for specific places or events are collected during the day and placed in a container (on the left) for Martin to select. The correct day in the diary is highlighted for Martin to record the chosen event(s). The supporting adult talks about Martin's choice with him and writes a comment if appropriate. As Martin learns to recognise pictures, the communication book can continue using pictures. Thus Martin is using objects and logos to communicate information to others.

Mini-enterprise

Visual information is equally important outside the classroom. Martin's year group has taken part in a mini-enterprise project involving cleaning cars and mini-buses as part of their work in relation to enterprise and entrepreneurial skills in Key Stage 3 (DfEE/QCA 1999b: 24). Martin learned to wash wheels, lights and registration plates as part of the project. This required visual information and organisation to help Martin to complete his tasks independently. Washing materials were provided in one bucket and rinsing water and cloth in a second. These were arranged to follow in a left to right sequence and also taught as a 'first . . . then . . .' routine, 'first wash, then rinse'. Coloured stickers were used to indicate which areas Martin should clean. Martin was taught to begin at the left and work his way round the vehicle looking for stickers. A 'finished' bucket was used by all pupils for materials they had used and were finished with.

Independent tasks: numeracy

This activity also led to developing individual tasks for Martin that would enable him to practise and consolidate basic skills. For example, after collecting payment for cleaning cars, Martin

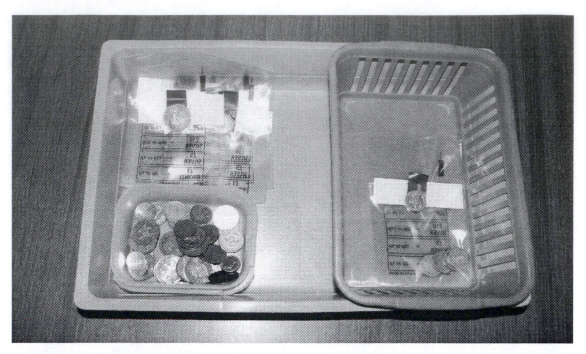

Figure 7.6: Independent numeracy task, linked to mini-enterprise project.

sorted coins into moneybags in order to take them to the bank (Figure 7.6). This task allows Martin to reinforce his ability to recognise coins (DfEE 1999: 68), within a meaningful, real-life context linked to the mini-enterprise project. The materials are organised in a tray for Martin to work from left to right. Coloured tape clarifies where to open individual moneybags.

Visual information for Martin focuses upon visual organisation and clarity, rather than extra visual instructions that he will not yet understand. Some pupils will be able to follow simple, to complex, visual directions that help them to understand and access lessons. The following examples illustrate the use of picture instructions for independent work, group work and playtimes.

CASE STUDY
Picture instructions

Some pupils understand pictures and photographs and can follow picture instructions. Ricky is six years old, has ASD and learning difficulties and attends specialist autism provision within a school for children with a range of special educational needs. He uses a photograph schedule (Chapter 3) and a colour/shape matching work system (Chapter 6). Additional visual information is used to help Ricky to work independently and to follow visual instructions in group and class lessons. Ricky has daily independent work times for practising learnt skills and to reinforce specific concepts. He completes tasks relating to core subjects on a daily basis. In addition, topic-related tasks are structured for foundation subjects and for activities such as structured play.

Literacy

During independent work time in the literacy hour, Ricky completes tasks that are designed to provide him with opportunities to consolidate learnt skills linked to the literacy lesson or to individual targets. For example, following a school trip to a local farm park, and a subsequent lesson based upon a story about farm animals, Ricky works independently matching pictures of farm animals that appear in the story (Figure 7.7).

Figure 7.7: Independent task: literacy.

This task is organised in a left to right sequence for Ricky within a folder. He has been taught to match the photos following the top to bottom sequence on each page. The left to right and top to bottom routines reinforce reading direction and the task also reinforces Ricky's knowledge of how books work. As Ricky begins to recognise symbols, the task can progress to matching symbols to photographs. Further progress may lead to a similar structured activity to help Ricky to construct his own story about farm animals with adult support, with a selection of coloured pictures to choose from and a prepared template on which Ricky can place his pictures (Figure 7.8). The adult can then discuss appropriate captions with him. Later he may write his own caption using symbols, achieving P5 (QCA 2001c: 31).

The task is organised for Ricky and the use of Velcro ensures that his materials stay in place once selected. Thus Ricky is provided with opportunities in literacy 'to write about events in personal experience linked to a variety of familiar incidents from stories' (DfEE 1998: 21) within a structured activity drawing upon his own experience and using familiar resources.

Although Ricky is not yet writing the story himself, he is being supported to make a book using pictures and to offer suggestions for what to write. The visual template helps Ricky to organise himself to construct the book as independently as possible. This can be extended by providing different visual templates for the book layout from which Ricky can choose.

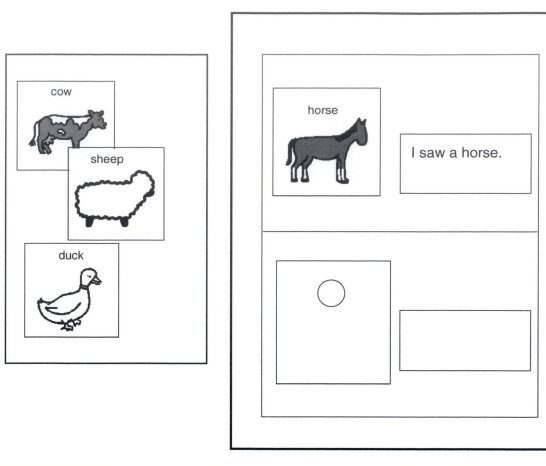

Figure 7.8: Visual structure: story composition.

Design and technology

Similar levels of visual information are used for other subject-based lessons. For example in design and technology, Ricky is learning to 'assemble, join and combine materials and components' (DfEE/QCA 1999a: 92). Visual information is provided as picture instructions for Ricky to follow (Figure 7.9). Without these visual instructions, Ricky loses interest or assembles materials in repetitive ways.

This activity is visually organised from left to right with a picture instruction for Ricky to follow. Ricky can be encouraged to become more flexible in his use of different components by following different picture instructions. For some pupils it is possible to incorporate elements of choice within the picture instructions, for example by omitting the colour of some components so that the pupil still has instructions for the model but must decide on some of the colours. Similarly, by adding question marks the pupil must decide which components to use for parts of the model. In this way, the pupil can be encouraged to solve simple problems and develop early thinking skills (QCA 2001b: 12) within the security of the visual structure that has been provided (Figure 7.10).

Once Ricky can follow visual instructions, he can be encouraged to play alongside others. For example, picture instructions for assembling a variety of resources can be made available in the play area with the appropriate materials. Ricky is taught to play alongside another pupil with shared materials, but following his own visual instructions. The LSA can then focus on the social learning that is a priority for Ricky, rather than only helping him to organise the equipment.

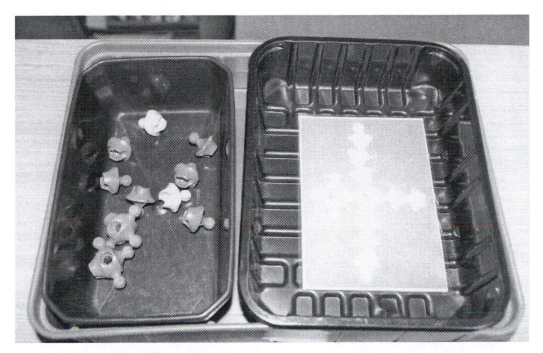

Figure 7.9: Picture instructions: assembling, joining and combining materials and components.

Figure 7.10: Visual instructions: early problem solving and thinking skills.

Art and design

Visual information can also be incorporated into class lessons such as art. Ricky's class spent some time investigating patterns and the use of black and white. A variety of 'greyscale' visual images provided visual directions for producing patterns (for example see Figure 7.11).

Figure 7.11: Visual information: art

Pupils were encouraged to choose an image that they could then use as a guide for their work. Without the visual directions, most of the pupils would have daubed paint repetitively and not had the opportunity to produce patterns. Following the use of the directions, some pupils began to develop their own patterns.

Playtimes

Visual information is equally important at other times. During playtimes Ricky follows a photograph work system to indicate which activities to complete. Without the use of the work system, Ricky wanders aimlessly and does not initiate nor engage in any activities. Although he likes to wander, if left for too long he will become distressed and frustrated. By providing a work system he can be guided to a range of activities, including a time for wandering. These instructions are followed top to bottom; Ricky follows the instructions, removing each photograph when it is time to finish the activity (indicated by a lunchtime supervisor ringing a bell). A typical break time might include a sequence such as 'bike, basketball, walk'. Further visual information helps Ricky to participate in the activities. For example, a 'road layout' on the playground clarifies where to ride his bike (without this he rides his bike over the field, which is designated for football). When Ricky joins the basketball activity a list of tokens are stuck on the wall, indicating how many turns he will have. In addition, a 'your turn' picture card is given to each pupil when it is their turn. As Ricky has a turn, he places a token in a bucket; when all the tokens are gone from the wall and are in the 'finished' bucket, Ricky knows his turn is over. As Ricky becomes more familiar and confident with a range of activities, the instructions can be developed to include an element of choice. In this way, visual instructions are providing Ricky with opportunities to encourage him to begin to make simple choices. Playtimes can be opportune times for pupils to learn the key skill of 'working with others' within a structured play context. Visual information can help pupils to understand what to do and reduces confusion, important precursors to learning to play alongside and with others.

Additional visual information is provided for pupils depending upon their level of visual cognition. Visual organisation and instructions are individualised and can provide flexible ways of providing structure for a wide range of activities. Some pupils will also understand symbols or icons and their understanding can be greatly enhanced by this type of information to supplement verbal directions.

CASE STUDY
Symbol instructions

Leila is nine years old and has autism and learning difficulties. She attends specialist provision, within a mainstream school, for pupils with special educational needs, two of whom have ASD. Leila uses a part-day symbol schedule and number matching work system. Additional visual information clarifies important information within a task, helps Leila to organise tasks and provides symbol instructions to identify the sequence of steps she needs to take in order to complete a task. The following examples illustrate how visual information is presented to help Leila to increase her understanding in group and class lessons, to work independently and to understand the sequence and purpose of specific activities such as assembly.

Literacy

During the literacy hour Leila has symbol instructions to supplement the teacher's verbal directions. Symbols are also used when Leila is working with others. During a literacy lesson that focuses upon writing, Leila works within Key Stage 1 programmes of study for English. She is asked to write a letter to her mum about a recent residential trip linked to writing and composition, i.e. 1b 'sequence events and recount them in appropriate detail', 1c 'put their ideas into sentences', 1d 'use a clear structure to organise their writing' (DfEE/QCA 1999a: 48). Leila works with another pupil and a LSA. Both pupils use a visually structured ideas sheet to help them to recount events (Figure 7.12). Following this, the LSA helps Leila to complete her letter by referring to her ideas sheet and inserting symbols and words on a prepared letter using the computer.

Science

In science, Leila's class completed a series of lessons on 'growing' including growing beans, observing the stages of growth, recognising the parts of the plant and that the roots grow in the dark while the green leaves need light (science 3a, 3b DfEE/QCA 1999a: 79). During one lesson, Leila worked with another pupil planting beans into individual pots. Symbol instructions were used by both pupils to help them complete the activity. The worksheet followed a top to bottom, numbered sequence and key points and teaching points were clarified by highlighting. The use of these instructions allowed Leila and her peer to be independent in carrying out each stage of the task. Without the instructions, Leila would need the LSA to spend time with her on sequencing the task and organisation, rather than on emphasising the teaching points.

In addition, prior to the lesson, Leila was allocated the task of giving out materials to pairs of children. A symbol list (Figure 7.13) enabled her to fulfil this task without becoming confused by the large number of materials to deal with. The list was used to collect sets of materials to then give out to her peers, one of Leila's individual targets relating to developing her social skills. The list reduced anxieties relating to organisation and means Leila can concentrate on the social target she is working towards.

Developing independence

Visual information can be used to help pupils to develop independent working skills across the range of subjects. Tasks that are designed to be completed independently may relate to class

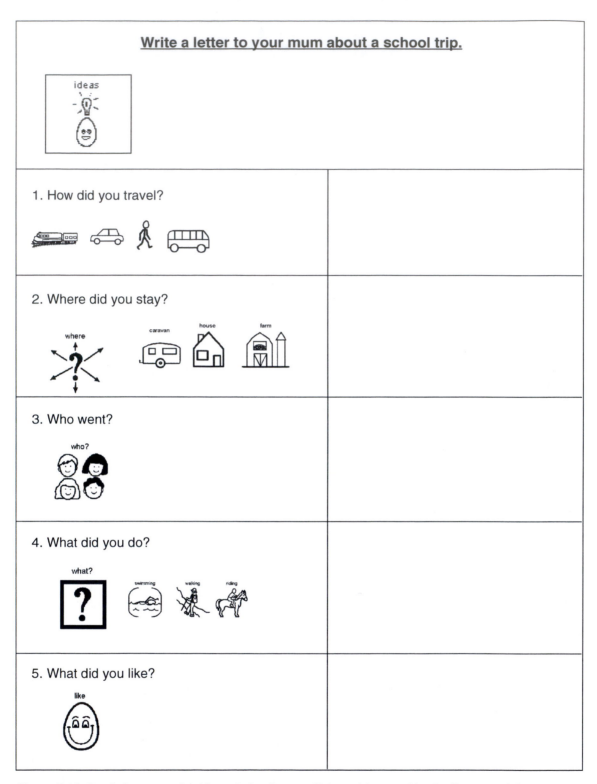

Figure 7.12: Symbols: generating ideas during literacy. (Adapted from an idea by Berger and Gross 1999: 50.)

lessons or to individual targets. Such tasks should be monitored and pupil achievement recorded to ensure that pupils are offered opportunities to consolidate their learning but also make progress. Independent tasks will be structured taking into account organisation of resources, clarity of what is required and instructions to help pupils understand what to do.

Give each pair of children	Jane Sally	Tim Sam	Mark Amy	Gita Alex	Tina Beth
 2 plant pots					
 a bag of compost					
 1 scoop					
 2 beans					

Figure 7.13: Symbol list: working with others and social skills.

In order to reinforce the sequence of growing, the class sequenced pictures of the stages of growth. A LSA structured an activity for Leila to complete independently (Figure 7.14). This task makes use of symbolic pictures that Leila can match following a left to right, top to bottom sequence. Numbers also help Leila to complete the sequence correctly. This task was one of several designed to consolidate Leila's understanding of the growth of green plants.

Similar tasks can be made for pupils to consolidate their learning in other areas. When Leila's class were looking at skeletons (science 2e, DfEE/QCA 1999a: 85), the LSA made a task that Leila and others could complete independently to rehearse and reinforce their recognition of body parts in relation to the skeleton (Figure 7.15). The task is organised in a tray with prepared cut-out body parts; Velcro is used to ensure the pieces stay in place – this is important for ensuring that the work can be checked later. If Leila had been given the worksheet and had been required to cut out the body parts and stick them to the skeleton, she would have become disorganised and upset and would have needed considerable help. This would probably have distracted her from the relevant information relating to the task and she may well have focused entirely on organising materials rather than on the task objectives. This task allows Leila to complete the work independently without becoming

Figure 7.14: Independent task:
science – green plants.

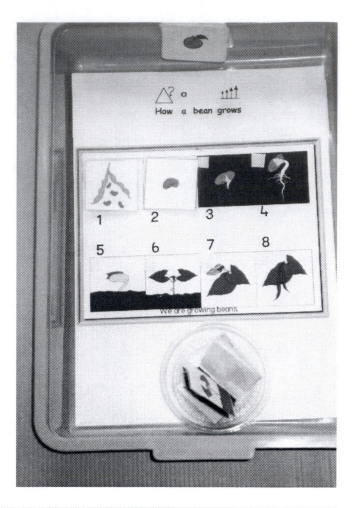

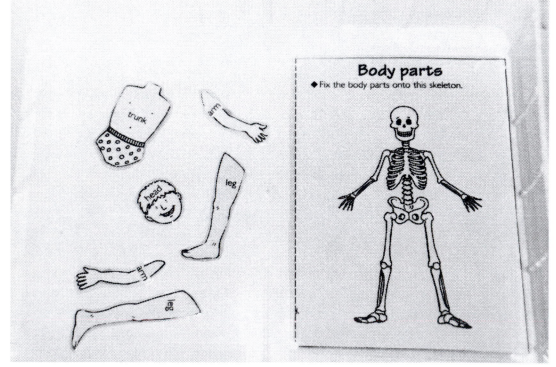

Figure 7.15: Independent task: science – the skeleton.

distressed and enabling her to focus on matching body parts to the skeleton rather than on organising herself.

Physical education

Visual instructions can be incorporated into PE lessons for pupils with ASD and others. During a series of lessons focusing on travelling Leila follows visual instructions (Figure 7.16) to help her to perform gymnastic activities as indicated in the PE programmes of study for Key Stage 1: 8a 'perform basic skills in travelling . . .', 8b 'develop the range of their skills and actions', 'choose and link skills and actions in short movement phrases' (DfEE/QCA 1999a: 131).

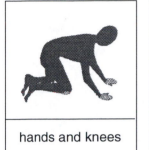 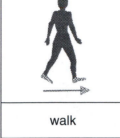  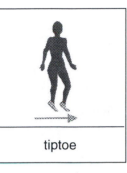

| hands and knees | walk | bottom: push with hands | tiptoe |

Figure 7.16: Visual instructions: PE.

Initially visual cues were used during a lesson using low level apparatus arranged in a circuit. Visual cues were placed at each piece of apparatus to indicate how to travel, for example along a bench, and Leila was taught how to follow these instructions. As pupils become familiar with the visual cues, they can be varied during the lesson and can be extended to encourage pupils to follow a sequence of cues to link movements and/or to incorporate choice, encouraging creative thinking and imagination (Figure 7.17).

| tiptoe | what next? | skip |

Figure 7.17: Visual directions: choice and decision making – PE.

Encouraging early thinking skills: PSHE

Visual information can also be used to encourage early thinking skills, such as remembering (QCA 2001b: 12), across the curriculum. For example, Leila is 'developing personal autonomy' (QCA 2001f: 9) in relation to making decisions in the community. Following a community visit, a LSA discovered that she is unsure of which toilets she should use and frequently wandered into the 'gents'. Subsequently a series of community visits were set up to teach Leila to find the 'ladies' in a variety of contexts. The LSA made a set of activities depicting the sequence of a variety of visits to encourage Leila to plan and also to decide which toilet symbol she should look for.

| We are going to the shopping centre. | I will buy | We are going to the cafeteria. | I will buy | We will go to the toilet. | Which toilet? |

Figure 7.18: Visual information to encourage early thinking skills and personal autonomy – PSHE.

Figure 7.18 shows one such sequence (a selection of symbols are provided from which the pupil may choose). This activity is completed with the LSA and another pupil before going on a visit. Leila is encouraged to decide what she will buy and record her decision using a symbol. She then selects the symbol for the toilet she should use. The completed task is taken by Leila on her trip to remind her of her planning. The structure of this activity allows Leila to develop planning skills and to make decisions relating to everyday problems.

Other aspects of the curriculum

Visual cues also help Leila in a wide range of other ways. For example, during assemblies, she would become anxious about what would happen and often asked to leave part way through. Leila's teacher felt that Leila's anxiety was partly due to her lack of understanding about the organisation of assembly and when it would finish so that she could return to her classroom. Hence, an assembly book was provided for her to understand the sequence of assembly and when it would finish (Figure 7.19).

| assembly | listen to music | light the candle | listen | sing | pray | blow out | finished |

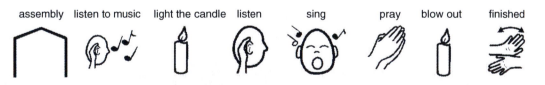

Figure 7.19: Visual cues: assembly book (one icon per page).

Leila was given a personal copy of the book, fastened with a treasury tag so that the order can be changed according to the assembly. A large version was also used for the whole school as it was felt that other children would also benefit from being able to follow the sequence. The person leading assembly orders the book according to their plan and a pupil is selected at the beginning of each assembly to turn the pages as appropriate (Leila loves this job). This has now been extended to include the use of picture and symbol information to help pupils to better understand the content of assembly.

Monitoring behaviour and following rules

Symbols are also used to visually remind Leila of appropriate behaviour in different lessons and contexts. For example, to remind Leila (and other pupils) not to call out or interrupt, a symbol for 'hands up' is placed on the whiteboard at appropriate times during lessons (Figure 7.20).

The teacher finds this is a useful reminder that Leila is more likely to respond to, cutting down the need for

Figure 7.20: Visual cue: reminder to raise hand rather than call out.

hand up

constant verbal reminders that quickly become 'nagging'. This strategy is easily individualised for other pupils, for example by holding up a cut-out hand on a stick as illustrated for 'David' in the video for supporting pupils with special educational needs in the literacy hour (DfEE 2000). Similar symbol cues can be used to remind pupils about how they should be behaving or what they should be doing (Figure 7.21).

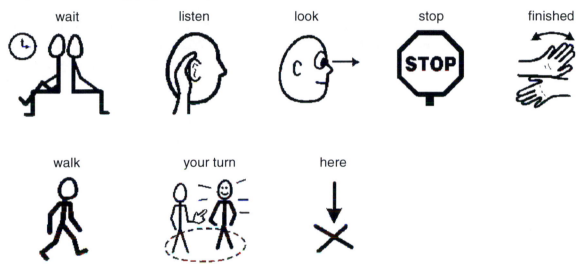

Figure 7.21: Examples of symbols used as visual reminders of appropriate behaviour.

Symbol cues visually remind pupils of the important aspects during a lesson and are helpful when they become distracted. Individual symbols can be given to individual pupils by support staff to remind them of expectations for behaviour. They can be used during lessons, at playtimes and lunchtimes, during assemblies and so on.

Visual information can be individualised to incorporate combinations of symbols and words for some pupils. Different pupils will require different levels of symbols depending upon their reading and comprehension ability. For Leila, the emphasis is on the symbols while for David, the emphasis is on written words, supplemented by symbols.

CASE STUDY
Symbol/word instructions

David attends a specialist school for pupils with ASD. He is 11 years old and is preparing for transition to secondary provision with the support of a LSA. David follows his symbol/word schedule independently and takes a portable version with him to the secondary school (Chapter 5). Additional visual directions help David to complete work independently, to increase his understanding during class lessons and to increase his independence in self-care areas. David follows simple written directions with symbols to supplement and increase his understanding and to encourage investigation and problem solving.

Science

David's class has been learning about electricity during their work on physical processes and David has joined in supported activities to learn how to complete simple circuits (science: 1a, 1b, 1c, DfEE/QCA 1999a: 88). David can now construct circuits independently following written directions, with symbols to ensure understanding (Figure 7.22). Conventional symbols are placed alongside the symbols David is familiar with. Similar directions can be used to encourage him to investigate what happens when components in the circuit are changed, making bulbs brighter or dimmer, or to introduce buzzers or motors. Parts of the directions can be replaced with a '?' or a choice. By providing key visual information with elements of choice, or questions, David is encouraged to solve problems and investigate 'what happens if . . . ?'.

Independent tasks: mathematics

David has particular strengths in this curriculum area and is able to be included in a mainstream class for mathematics and numeracy lessons. Nevertheless, he still benefits from visual information to highlight, clarify and draw his attention to key points. For example, in a lesson focusing on ratio (DfEE 1999: 26), as part of the lesson pupils are given a table to complete missing numbers using the ratio 1:2. David's worksheet has additional visual information to ensure that he focuses on the relevant concepts. David's interest in fast food and 'buy one get one free' offers is used to increase motivation (Figure 7.23). Key points and spaces for David's answers are highlighted for clarity and additional instructions remind him which operations he needs to use. A visual cue also reminds him to put up his hand if he needs help.

Religious education

David's teacher adapted the DfEE/QCA (2000b) Key Stage 2 scheme of work for RE for the class, following guidelines for teaching pupils with learning difficulties (QCA 2001g: 11). During a period of work based upon the Christian celebration of Easter, David's class visited a local church to find artefacts and pictures that link with the Easter story. David and his peers were provided with visual information to help focus their attention on relevant objects in the church. Without this visual information, David would have become overwhelmed by the environment and would probably have forgotten what he was supposed to be looking for.

In addition, a symbol/word dictionary was prepared to help David and other pupils to develop their understanding of the key vocabulary used for the topic (Figure 7.24). This dictionary was referred to during a series of lessons to draw pupils' attention to key concepts in the story. While

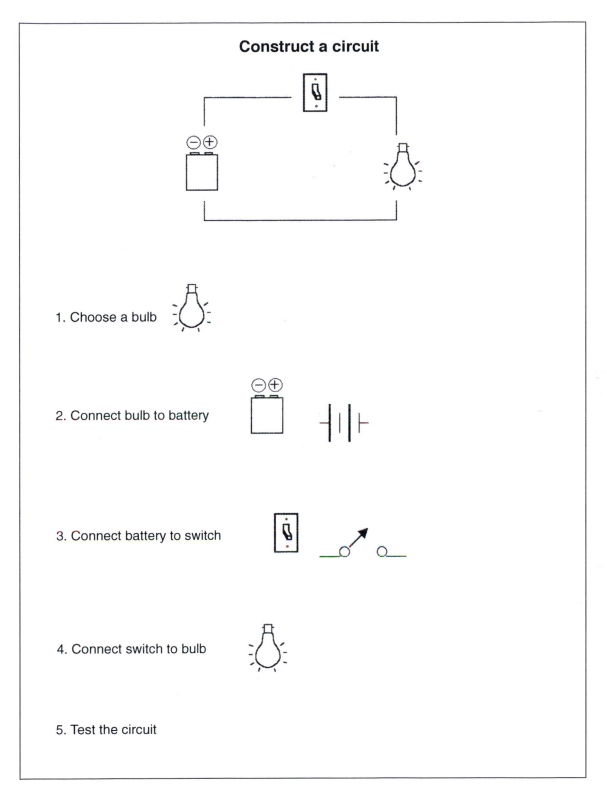

Construct a circuit

1. Choose a bulb

2. Connect bulb to battery

3. Connect battery to switch

4. Connect switch to bulb

5. Test the circuit

Figure 7.22: Visual instructions: science.

Ratio 1:2

For every **1 burger** that you buy, you receive **2 drinks** free

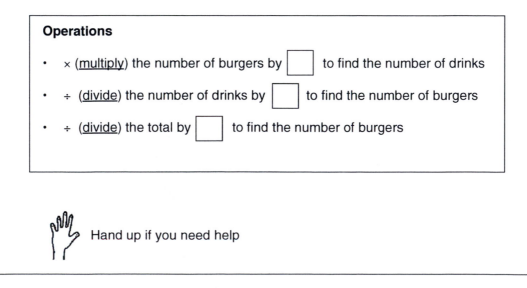

Fill in the table using the **ratio 1:2**

Burgers	Drinks	Total (burgers and drinks)
1	2	3
2	?	6
5	10	?
20	?	?
60	?	?
?	160	?
?	?	300

Operations

- × (<u>multiply</u>) the number of burgers by [   ] to find the number of drinks

- ÷ (<u>divide</u>) the number of drinks by [   ] to find the number of burgers

- ÷ (<u>divide</u>) the total by [   ] to find the number of burgers

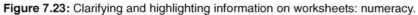 Hand up if you need help

Figure 7.23: Clarifying and highlighting information on worksheets: numeracy.

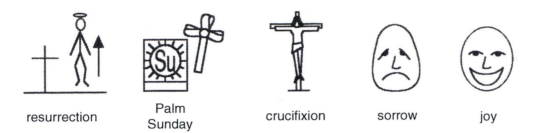

| resurrection | Palm Sunday | crucifixion | sorrow | joy |

Figure 7.24: Examples of symbols used in a symbol/word dictionary: RE.

David still has difficulties understanding the concepts of RE lessons, this example shows how visual information can help to increase meaning as far as possible.

Personal, social and health education

Despite his academic ability in some areas of the curriculum, David often becomes confused by everyday self-care tasks and as a result he has an individual target in the area of PSHE relating to personal hygiene (PSHE 3b, DfEE/QCA 1999a: 137). David was encouraged to follow symbol/word directions to complete routine self-care tasks because he had been observed trying to dress before he was dry and putting clothes on in an incorrect sequence; this caused him enormous distress. David also needed to learn to use deodorant appropriately. One of his half-termly targets was to follow visual directions in order to dry and dress himself in the correct sequence following swimming and to use deodorant. Symbol/word directions were introduced following a top to bottom list (Figure 7.25). Some words do not need symbols as David can complete this step independently. The symbol for deodorant is larger than other symbols as this is a new step for David. The directions were put onto a laminated postcard that David kept in his swimming bag. He learnt to follow these directions and was able to use them with his parents when the family went swimming at weekends. David may eventually learn the routine of drying and dressing and may not need these directions in the future; however, some pupils will need to keep directions such as these in order to maintain independence.

Get dry

dry head and face

dry neck

dry chest and tummy

dry arms

dry back

dry legs

dry feet

deodorant

Get dressed

pants

vest

t-shirt

trousers

jumper

socks

shoes

Figure 7.25: Symbol/word directions: PSHE – personal hygiene.

Some pupils with ASD will be able to cope with written, and increasingly complex, instructions. Such pupils may well respond to verbal directions, but may become adult dependent. Written information reduces this dependence and increases the pupil's autonomy.

CASE STUDY
Written instructions

Sarah is nine years old and has a diagnosis of ASD. She attends her local primary school and is supported in Year 4 by a LSA for 75 per cent of lessons. Sarah has good expressive language, although this can mask her difficulties with comprehension. She has poor organisational and sequencing abilities and is unable to recall sequences of instructions. Sarah reads well and this strength has proven to be very useful in providing her with visual information. She follows written information, together with occasional symbols to help highlight or increase meaning when needed. The following examples illustrate how written information is used to help Sarah to work independently, to increase her understanding during class lessons and to remind her of social rules.

Literacy and ICT

In Chapter 6, Sarah's work system was illustrated to show how she can be more organised when working with peers during a literacy lesson, incorporating ICT. Sarah's class prepared a report for a school newsletter about their recent sports day, working within Key Stage 2 programmes of study (Writing 1a, 1e, 2e: 56; Speaking and listening 3a, 3b: 50; ICT 1a, 1b, 2a, 3b, 4b: 100–1; DfEE/QCA 1999a). A 'jigsaw' approach was used to divide several tasks between groups (Rose 1991) and Sarah's group was responsible for selecting and editing photographs, writing appropriate captions and reporting back to the whole class. Written instructions were prepared to remind Sarah how to use the ICT software to select and edit photographs and to add her captions (Figure 7.26).

These instructions were also used by other pupils and were kept with a bank of similar ones that could be used for other software. The instructions are laminated so that Sarah can use a dry-wipe pen to check off each instruction as she completes it. Note that Sarah is familiar with saving work and does not need instructions for where to save her file or what to call it; these instructions could be added for pupils who need them. This example shows how written instructions help Sarah to develop thinking skills, for example information processing skills requiring pupils to 'locate and collect relevant information'.

Selecting and inserting photos
Writing captions

1. Open **Word**
2. Select **new page**
3. Click on **insert**
4. Click on **picture**
5. Click on **from file**
6. Click on the C drive
7. Click on the folder for **sports day**
8. Select the file you want to look at – double click on the name
9. Click on **text box**
10. **Draw** text box
11. Write **caption** for the photo

Repeat steps 3–11 to insert more photos

12. **Save** your work and **print**

Figure 7.26: Written instructions: ICT.

Sarah also had a written reminder to help her to work with her peers, thus offering strategies to enable her to work more effectively with others (Figure 7.27). This reminder is written on the back of Sarah's instructions for the lesson, so that she can refer to them when she needs to. Similar instructions are used when Sarah works with others during other lessons.

Visual information during whole-class teaching

During whole-class introductions to literacy, Sarah often has a prepared written vocabulary sheet to help her to focus on the relevant and important aspects of the lesson. For example, in sentence level work, Sarah's class was identifying adverbs with the suffix ly and during one lesson the teacher showed the class some examples of classifying adverbs as indicated in the National Literacy Strategy: Framework for teaching (Grammatical awareness 4, DfEE 1998: 38). Sarah's teacher and the LSA discussed the lesson and the LSA prepared a vocabulary sheet for Sarah to refer to during the whole-class discussion (Figure 7.28).

Working with other children

- <u>listen</u> to what others have to say
- <u>take turns</u> in the conversation
- <u>speak</u> (don't shout – it hurts their ears)
- <u>ask questions</u> when it is <u>your turn</u>
- offer <u>suggestions</u> and say what you think when it is <u>your turn</u>
- try to say <u>positive and kind</u> words about other children's ideas

<u>Remember</u> it is your turn when someone looks at you and pauses, or if they ask you a question. If you forget, someone will give you a 'your turn' card.

Figure 7.27: Written reminder: working with others.

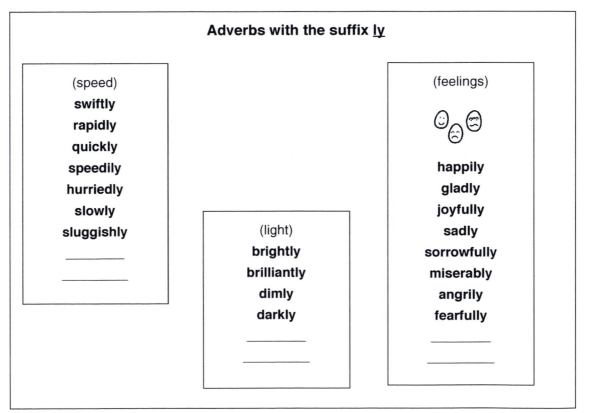

Adverbs with the suffix <u>ly</u>

(speed)
swiftly
rapidly
quickly
speedily
hurriedly
slowly
sluggishly
_____
_____

(light)
brightly
brilliantly
dimly
darkly
_____
_____

(feelings)
happily
gladly
joyfully
sadly
sorrowfully
miserably
angrily
fearfully
_____
_____

Figure 7.28: Written vocabulary sheet: literacy.

Having a prepared sheet helps Sarah to maintain her attention during the lesson. If she is distracted the LSA can remind her to use her vocabulary sheet to regain her attention. Important elements of the information are highlighted to draw Sarah's attention, for example the suffix ly is highlighted, the symbol for 'feelings' is used to increase meaning and spaces are left for Sarah to add any others suggested during the lesson.

Finally, Sarah's LSA and teacher always have highlighter pens in their pockets as one very quick way of drawing Sarah's attention to important and relevant information on worksheets is to highlight it. For example, 'small' words on a worksheet may be critical but may be missed by Sarah; highlighting words such as 'or', 'and' helps to draw Sarah's attention to the word and to then follow directions successfully. Highlighting also proved successful during shared reading when the teacher chose individual pupils to read aloud sections of text to the class. Sarah would become increasingly anxious about whether she would be chosen, and if chosen which section she would read. Consequently, she disrupted the reading with repetitive questions, she would not be able to listen to others reading and sometimes she would become distressed and have to leave the lesson. Sarah's teacher now highlights a section of text for Sarah if she is to be chosen. This way she knows in advance if she is to read aloud or not; she also knows which section she will read. This strategy of clarifying for Sarah the requirements of the activity reduced her anxiety and resulted in her being able to join in shared reading.

History

Pupils who read instructions may also need additional symbols at times to increase meaning. Anxiety may result in the pupils becoming 'de-skilled' in reading and understanding and in some instances this may be helped by adding symbols. Pupils with ASD frequently have difficulties with some concepts. For example, understanding the past and concepts related to history can be particularly problematic. Sarah finds it difficult to distinguish events in the past from the present and certain historical topics cause her great anxiety. For example, when the class were learning about World War II in Britain, Sarah became obsessive and afraid that she would have to be evacuated to live with a different family. While drawing upon the programmes of study to plan history schemes of work, Sarah's teacher also placed emphasis on 'the passage of time', drawing upon the QCA guidance for teaching pupils with learning difficulties (QCA 2001h: 11) and the programmes of study relating to chronological understanding in the National Curriculum (DfEE/QCA 1999a: 104, 105). Sarah's teacher developed with the class a written timeline for events in the recent, then increasingly distant past to help Sarah and her peers to develop their sense of the passing of time (Figure 7.29).

1939– 1944	1945	1952	1969	2000	2001 last year	Last month	Last week	Yester- day		Today
World War II	VE day (victory in Europe)	Corona- tion Queen Elizabeth II	Man landed on the moon	Millen- nium	'Harry Potter' film released	Queen's golden jubilee	Sports day	School party		School ends for summer

← ───

History   In the past   **Finished**   **Here and now**

Figure 7.29: Visual timeline: history.   **Present**

A timeline was hung from the classroom ceiling and as pupils learnt about new events they pegged them onto the line in the appropriate place. Sarah kept her own laminated version so that she could update it on a daily basis. The distinction between past and present is highlighted and clarified, with an emphasis on events in the past being finished. Although Sarah still needs support from the LSA during history lessons, she is becoming less anxious and confused about the distinction between past and present – a crucial first step in developing historical under-standing.

Science

Written instructions are used by Sarah in a range of subject areas. These instructions clarify the task, but can also emphasise specific aspects that may be challenging such as 'investigating'.

During a science lesson on magnetism, Sarah follows written directions, supplementing the teacher's verbal instructions (DfEE/QCA 1999a: 88). Scientific enquiry and investigation are crucial aspects of the lesson that may be challenging for Sarah.

 **1. Choose (4)**	paper wood stone metal ? ?
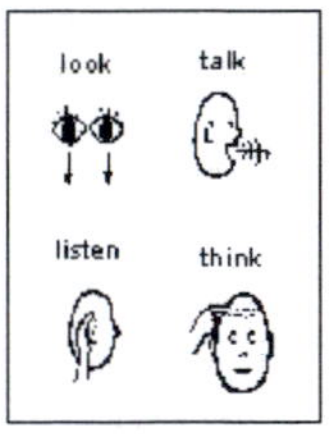 **2. Investigate**	Which materials are magnetic?
 **3. Record**	Put a <u>tick</u> next to the <u>magnetic materials</u>. Put a <u>cross</u> next to materials that are <u>not magnetic</u>.
 **4. Discuss**	Bring your work to the group to talk about what you found out.

Figure 7.30: Visual instructions to encourage investigation.

Symbols are incorporated with her written directions to remind Sarah of what she needs to do in order to investigate, record and communicate her findings (Figure 7.30). These symbols highlight important information for Sarah. In particular, the symbol for 'investigate' is larger and incorporates what Sarah needs to do. Similar strategies can be used to encourage pupils to predict and research.

Visual instructions may remind pupils of the steps they carried out to complete a task in order to record what they did. They may also help them to begin to sequence their own set of instructions.

Design and technology: food technology

During a series of lessons, Sarah's class designed a set of menus to promote healthy eating, at the same time appealing to young children. The end of the project culminated in trying out their menus with children in the Reception class, thus covering a number of programmes of study relating to developing, planning and communicating ideas, working with tools, equipment and materials and evaluating products (DfEE/QCA 1999a: 94). Sarah's group decided to plan a dessert using different fruits. Written directions reminded Sarah of the social rules for discussing ideas in a group as she needs reminders to take turns in conversation and to listen to others' responses and suggestions (see Figure 7.27). Further directions helped Sarah and one peer to make their 'traffic light treat'. Sarah followed the written 'recipe' from top to bottom and used the smiley faces as a way of monitoring her progress through the sequence of steps (Figure 7.31).

Traffic light treat	
You need 1 kiwi fruit, 1 satsuma, 3 strawberries and some yoghurt.	 😊
1. Peel a kiwi fruit, slice and put into the bottom of a glass.	 😊
2. Peel the satsuma and place the segments on top of the kiwi fruit.	 😊
3. Remove the stalk from the strawberries, wash them and slice them in half; place them on top of the satsuma segments.	
4. Spread the yoghurt on the top.	
5. Arrange 1 strawberry, 2 satsuma segments and 1 slice of kiwi fruit on the top to look like a traffic light.	

Figure 7.31: Written instructions: food technology.

These directions are written onto a laminated card and the smiley faces are spiral bound on the right; Sarah turns them over to record her progress – this reduces organisational difficulties that may arise if she had to find a pencil and tick off each step. When the activity is finished, the board can be wiped clean and reused.

Sarah also used these instructions to help her to produce a similar set, with pictures, for the children in Reception to make their own dessert. She decided to add a '?' to part of the instructions to encourage the children to choose one type of fruit, showing that her own awareness of making choices and simple decision making is developing.

Other aspects of the curriculum

Sarah's teacher uses written cue cards in a similar way to Leila's symbol cues. For example, Sarah does not realise that when the teacher talks to the whole class, she is also talking to Sarah. During whole-class teaching, Sarah's teacher places a written cue card (Figure 7.32) on her desk to remind Sarah that she should listen.

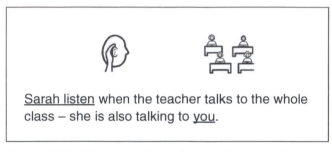

Sarah listen when the teacher talks to the whole class – she is also talking to you.

Figure 7.32: Written cue: listen during whole-class lessons.

Initially Sarah was handed her own personal cue card by the LSA; however the teacher found that by using one at the front, other children were also reminded to listen!

Written social rules

Written social rules are also used by Sarah's teacher to remind her about appropriate behaviour with peers. Sarah has a social rule written on her schedule reminding her to speak, not shout, when talking to peers (Figure 7.33).

Remember

Speak to other children in my group with a number 5 voice.

(1 = silence   **5 = speaking**   10 = shouting)

Figure 7.33: Written social rule.

The social rule is written onto Sarah's schedule as she is then provided with frequent opportunities to be reminded of it. This reduces 'verbal nagging' from adults and peers and when Sarah does shout, she is asked to read her rule on her schedule. Written directions such as these are important strategies to help pupils with ASD to develop social skills and understanding. PSHE and citizenship suggests that pupils should learn about relationships (e.g. 4a, DfEE/QCA 1999a: 140). Visual information, when used in conjunction with other strategies such as social stories (Gray 1998), can help pupils to develop in these important areas. Sarah had a social story that reminded her of why other people dislike it when she shouts; the social story included the rule that was written onto her schedule. Each time Sarah reads this reminder, it also reminds her of the social story that explains how people feel.

Like Sarah, other pupils with ASD will be able to read written directions to help them to access different aspects of the curriculum. For some pupils, written information will be critical in helping to reinforce understanding, reduce anxieties, increase organisational skills and improve communication with others.

CASE STUDY
Further uses of written instructions

Adam is 15 years old and has Asperger Syndrome. He attends a local mainstream secondary school and is studying for his GCSEs. Adam uses a student planner that incorporates a written daily schedule and his work system (Chapter 5). The teacher in charge of the learning support base found that Adam was helped significantly by visual information and written information in relation to a number of areas. These were linked less to understanding lesson content, as Adam was generally able to understand and learn in most lessons. Visual information was sometimes used to help prepare Adam for lessons where content may be problematic, but more often for providing him with information to reduce his anxieties, about what to expect and how to behave.

Preparing for lessons

Adam goes to the learning support base regularly. A small group of pupils have ASD and a specialist teacher teaches them at the base. The teacher is provided with advanced planning from Adam's subject teachers so that she can check to see if Adam will need any preparatory work before specific lessons. This may relate to lesson content or may be to prepare him for teaching approaches. The following example illustrates how visual information is provided to help Adam prepare for a geography lesson.

Geography

The theme of 'issues in physical geography' included some work on the Aswan High Dam as an example of a multi-purpose river scheme (adapted from Davidson 1996). Adam's class was to find out information relating to three questions and to prepare brief oral presentations for the next lesson. The teacher would introduce the lesson with key definitions, then give all students envelopes containing information relating to the three questions about the River Nile flood and the dam. Adam would be working firstly in a pair to find out information relating to one of the questions, then joining to work collaboratively with another pair to explain and discuss what they have found out. The support teacher felt that Adam needed some visual information to help him to achieve the learning objectives 'to extract and summarise information from text, cartoons and diagrams' and 'to work collaboratively in pairs and small groups'. Visual information was used to highlight key points to listen for in the lesson and key vocabulary with written definitions was discussed. The teacher also discussed the main teaching and learning processes with Adam in order to prepare him for working collaboratively and to remind him of the rules when working with others (Figure 7.34). Adam placed this written information in the geography section of his file to refer to during the lesson. He achieved the lesson objectives and worked with one peer successfully. Some adult support was still necessary to help him to collaborate as part of a small group – in this case the visual information also served as a reminder to the support assistant who could then provide Adam with consistent feedback and support.

<u>Geography Friday 8.45a.m.</u>

The Aswan High Dam

- <u>Listen</u> for the explanation of '<u>multi-purpose scheme</u>' – write it down.

- Write down the 3 questions written on the board.

- Work with Jane – look at the information on the card together, check which question you have (1 or 2).

- Highlight information on the card that relates to the question.

- Summarise this information in bullet points.

- Join with Tim and Jon. Explain the important points relating to your question. <u>Listen</u> to Tim and Jon explain their points.

- <u>Listen</u> to the teacher give directions to the whole class, <u>write down the directions</u>.

- Work with Jane, Tim and Jon to prepare a presentation on **'what problems has the dam caused?'** Use the information on your cards to find out important points. The presentation should last <u>5 minutes</u>. <u>Remember to listen</u> to Jane, Tim and Jon and to <u>take turns in the conversation</u>.

Figure 7.34: Written directions: preparation for geography lesson.

Homework

Adam uses similar written directions to ensure that he understands homework requirements, completes homework on time and hands it in to the correct teacher. In order to clarify the importance of completing homework the support teacher provided a diagram that clarifies how much time needs to be spent on homework, in proportion to class lessons, when studying for GCSEs (Figure 7.35).

Reducing anxiety

Initially, when Adam joined the secondary school he spent the majority of his time in the learning support base. His teacher used visual information to help him to begin to enter classrooms around the school building. One of the first challenges to overcome was Adam's intense fear of entering a classroom. Adam's teacher found that if he had something visual upon which he could focus, he could then enter a classroom with less anxiety. A small blue dot is placed on the floor by his desk at the front of the class (see Figure 4.6) where he can see it from the classroom doorway. Adam was taught to focus on the dot and rehearsed entering classrooms with a LSA. This enables Adam to enter classrooms more easily. In addition, it was agreed that he should be able to leave a lesson if he became overly anxious and return to the learning support base. A written reminder is placed at the front of his student planner and also on the outside of his pencil case and a number line helps him to monitor his anxiety level (Figure 7.36). The written direction reduces his anxieties as it reminds Adam what he could do if he becomes stressed and how to do it politely. This strategy was communicated to all subject staff to ensure a consistent approach – most staff are happy to use the strategy as the alternative was that Adam would begin to shout and disrupt the lesson.

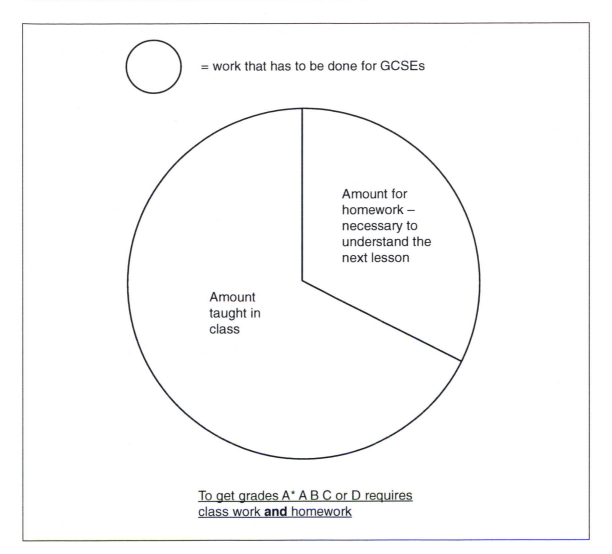

Figure 7.35: Visual information: homework requirements.

If I feel anxious I may raise my hand and tell the teacher 'I need to leave'. This is OK. I can go to learning support to find someone to talk to or I can sit and write down my worries.

1   5   10

Relaxed   A little anxious   Very anxious

'I need to leave'

Figure 7.36: Written reminder: reducing anxiety.

Geography and citizenship posed further anxieties for Adam when he was asked to regularly watch world news in relation to 'sustainable development and economic issues in geography' (QCA 2000: 13). Prior to this, Adam had been discouraged from watching the news as he became overly distressed by world affairs that he could not control. The support teacher introduced Adam gradually to a children's news programme, before watching the main news, and taught him to write down main points of interest and any worries he might have as a result of a news item. A further strategy involved completing a table identifying Adam's main worries, who is responsible for dealing with the problem and what Adam and his family or friends could do in response to the news item. For example when Adam became anxious about poverty and famine in Ethiopia, written strategies helped him to consider the issues and to identify possible solutions and responses (Figure 7.37).

News item	Issues this raises that cause me to worry	Who is reponsible for helping and what might they do?	What I could do
• Famine in Ethiopia due to drought and failing crops – evening news	• People are hungry and may die of starvation • What if the crops fail again?	• Politicians in Ethiopia and Africa may arrange to receive food donations from other countries • Other countries and charities may arrange to send seed, equipment and advisers to help people in Africa to grow crops again	• Give a donation to a charity that is helping the victims • The charity shop will sell things I take and the charity use the money to send food, seed, machinery and/or advisers to Africa

Figure 7.37: Written information to reduce anxieties: geography and citizenship.

Written bullet points help Adam to communicate his concerns and also to identify strategies to deal with them. He has learnt to complete a table, following columns from left to right and filling in information as bullet points. Any blanks are then discussed with Adam and his support teacher and his family who help him to complete the table.

Written directions are also used to help Adam prepare for unfamiliar events. For example, he was invited to attend a sixth form presentation evening to help him decide which AS and A level subjects he wished to study. Adam was taught to communicate his worries and anxieties to his support teacher by letter, and she would respond with a letter as he found a written response more meaningful and helpful. Adam wrote a note to the teacher listing his worries about the presentation evening as bullet points, including worries about what to wear, what time to arrive, who would be there, what would happen and when it would be appropriate to leave. Adam's teacher wrote a reply, and provided him with a plan (Figure 7.38).

Written lists such as these are immensely helpful in supporting Adam with new events and activities. Important points can be highlighted and clarified by underlining, colour, bold and so on. Despite Adam's good academic performance, he still needs visual information to ensure that he can fully access all opportunities. Without the written list, Adam would probably not have attended the presentation evening.

Extending visual information beyond school

Adam is a good example of a student who will require visual information in different settings, particularly as his world expands and he moves away from the security of school. Preparation for

- Do something relaxing (e.g. watch video, listen to music)

- Have dinner

- Change into appropriate **casual clothes**

- Ensure I have career's booklet with me before leaving in time to arrive at the school hall at **7.15p.m.**

- Sit in hall and use 'squeezy brain'

- The talk (given by Mr Taylor) willl begin at **7.30p.m.** and will last **approximately 30 minutes**

- Visit the various departments I am interested in. Walk and talk **calmly**

- Look at samples of work, talk to teachers and ask any questions I may have **(remember, wait for my turn)**

- Leave at approximately **9.15p.m. or before**

Figure 7.38: Visual instructions: preparation for sixth form presentation evening.

entering work placements, college courses and further and higher education will require the same level of visual information if Adam is to feel confident and independent in increasingly demanding settings. Visual information was used during Adam's work experience in a library and the following example illustrates the importance of continuing the structure as Adam prepares for life beyond school.

Work-related learning

Adam completed work experience in a local library, as this was an environment that he felt comfortable in and where he would be able to use his skills. Adam used a schedule and work system (Chapters 5 and 6) and in addition, further visual information was provided to help him to complete his jobs. The examples in Figure 7.39 illustrate instructions for replacing stock on the shelves and receiving returned books from customers.

Stock replacement

1. Find the book trolleys on the ground floor
2. Find the trolley with books 371–599
3. Take the trolley by lift to floor 2
4. Replace the books on the shelves using the classification numbers
5. Return to the ground floor and check schedule

Returns desk

1. Serve each customer one at a time – say good morning **or** good afternoon
2. Scan the bar code in each book
3. Check monitor to see if fee is due – tell customer the fee if they need to pay
4. Replace books on the trolley and say thank you to the customer

Figure 7.39: Written directions: work experience.

Similar instructions were used for photocopying and tidying the store cupboard. Adam's instructions also indicated what to do during breaks, who to tell when finished and so on. A written list of 'conversation openers' was also provided to help Adam initiate conversations with colleagues during break times. Adam completed the work experience very successfully, with one episode where he became anxious at having work checked. Written rules for who can check work and how he should respond overcame this particular challenge.

Conclusion

Visual information is an essential component of Structured Teaching. It can help to clarify important concepts, provide organisation for how to tackle tasks and provide directions to help pupils to complete their work. Visual information is one useful differentiation strategy when planning and preparing work for pupils with ASD. Clearly such information must be individualised; each pupil will have different requirements as what helps one pupil may not help another. This means it is impossible to provide structured lesson plans that can be copied for all other pupils. The examples given in this chapter illustrate the principles of using visual information as a teaching style, in response to preferred learning styles and individual needs. Visual information is provided to help individual pupils to understand what they are required to do and to increase the meaning of activities across the curriculum (Table 7.1).

Table 7.1: Access to the curriculum through use of visual information.

Curriculum area	Visual information promotes
Early Learning Goals	• Differentiation of teaching strategies taking into account individual learning needs and preferred learning styles
National Curriculum: Key Skills and Thinking skills	• Communication • Working with others • Problem solving • Information-processing skills • Enquiry skills • Creative-thinking skills
National Curriculum Core and Foundation Subjects	• Differentiation of teaching strategies taking into account individual learning needs and preferred learning styles
PSHE and citizenship	• Social skills and understanding • Monitoring behaviour
Enterprise and work-related learning	• Independence and self-reliance
Other aspects of the curriculum	• Independence and flexibility

As with all elements of Structured Teaching, visual information must be individualised for each pupil. Ongoing monitoring of the use of this information is critical to ensure that the most appropriate information is provided to ensure that teaching and learning are meaningful for the pupil. Visual information should be considered when planning lessons and activities for pupils with ASD, for developing appropriate behaviour, to increase flexibility and to enable pupils to be included in all aspects of school and community life. The four elements of Structured Teaching, physical structure, schedules, work systems and visual information, together provide essential strategies for pupils with ASD. When each of these areas is considered, structure can be provided that enables pupils to be included. While each element of Structured Teaching has been considered separately in this book, clearly if a pupil with ASD is to benefit from similar structured strategies, it is essential to consider all four elements in relation to the pupil's individual needs. The next chapter looks at how the different elements of structure combine to provide opportunities for pupils to learn and to be included.

8 Tying it all together

This book has reviewed the fundamentals of Division TEACCH's Structured Teaching approach and how it can be used to help pupils with ASD to access the curriculum. The authors have not taken any philosophical position about whether the National Curriculum is useful or if it should be used with pupils with ASD. Rather, the starting point for this presentation is that the National Curriculum exists as part of the whole curriculum to which all pupils are entitled. The whole curriculum should provide breadth and balance, at the same time responding to individual learning needs. Structured Teaching provides some excellent strategies for helping pupils with ASD to better access the curriculum; some of these productive strategies have been described in order to illustrate how the approach can facilitate curriculum access.

There are four essential components of Division TEACCH's Structured Teaching approach: physical structure, visual schedules, work systems and the visual structure of specific activities or tasks. Each of these parts of Structured Teaching helps pupils with autism to access the curriculum in meaningful and important ways. In Chapter 4, physical structure is described and explained. Individualising pupil work areas is consistent with DfES (2001a) statutory guidelines suggesting that some pupils benefit from workstations in quiet parts of the classroom or even outside of it. The National Curriculum encourages teachers to overcome potential barriers to learning, and to create effective learning environments for all pupils (DfEE/QCA 1999a, b). For those with ASD, a clear, visually organised environment is the first step in making classrooms meaningful and manageable for them by creating a predictable environment, either in mainstream or specialised settings. For many of these pupils, this will be their first step toward accessing the curriculum and is an important way of overcoming a major barrier to learning.

In addition to increasing understanding, the physical environment can also help reduce anxiety, which has a direct impact on a pupil's behaviour and ability to learn. For example, the Early Learning Goals relating to personal, social and emotional development include the need for pupils to develop positive dispositions and attitudes, behaviour and self-control (DfEE/QCA 2000a). These areas are often challenging for pupils with ASD and are often priority areas of learning. A clear, consistent and predictable physical structure can promote these goals by reducing anxiety.

Working with others is identified as a key skill in the National Curriculum (DfEE/QCA 1999a, b) and again is an area that can be challenging for pupils with ASD. The physical space, and structure of that space, can be important in promoting the conditions that allow pupils with ASD to interact and work more effectively with others.

Organisation and study skills are identified as additional key skills in the guidance for teaching pupils with learning difficulties (QCA 2001b). Clear boundaries that minimise distractions can help pupils with ASD to develop the organisational and study skills that are needed to access all subjects across the curriculum. Teaching pupils to manage their own behaviour is another of the personal and social skills emphasised in this guidance. The physical structure of the classroom can be a major factor in keeping pupils with ASD calm, thus promoting this objective. Making meaningful choices is also influenced by a physical environment that makes choices clearer, and helps pupils with ASD to understand what is available to them.

Physical structure can help pupils to progress toward full participation in classroom activities. For example, defining areas with the use of small portable screens or coloured tape can be useful in a wide variety of contexts. Screens, or visual demarcation, break up space, which is helpful for pupils with ASD. These dividers can also clarify what is expected in certain areas and help pupils with ASD to concentrate.

In summary, effective physical structure of the classroom can promote Early Learning Goals relating to personal, social and emotional development. Physical structure can help pupils to share space and work with others as a key skill embedded within the National Curriculum. Organisation and study skills, personal and social skills and self-management of behaviour, identified in the QCA (2001b) guidance for teaching pupils with learning difficulties, can also be encouraged through the use of physical structure.

The second area of Structured Teaching, reviewed in Chapter 5, is visual schedules. These daily schedules provide visual information informing pupils with ASD what will occur during their day and in what sequence. Visual schedules allow pupils to anticipate and understand what will be happening to them and when. Schedules can be developed so that they are meaningful for pupils with ASD at any level of functioning.

Daily schedules help pupils with ASD to access the curriculum in a number of ways. The use of visual schedules can further National Curriculum goals by reducing confusion, and increasing flexibility, thereby encouraging access to a wider range of activities. Schedules also help increase curriculum access by: improving communication; improving understanding of what will happen, when, and where; and improving transitions from lesson to lesson. Schedules are important because they can improve the general understanding of what goes on at school.

Curriculum Guidance for the Foundation Stage (DfEE/QCA 2000a) identifies personal, social and emotional development as one of the Early Learning Goals, and includes developing a positive disposition to learn, as well as self-confidence and motivation. Schedules help promote these goals by teaching young children what is happening in their environment. The use of visual schedules and positive routines offers strategies for developing important skills identified in this area of learning.

Schedules can also help with transitions. They provide a consistent way for pupils with ASD to change activities and a meaningful way for them to understand what is coming next. Schedules are very effective for facilitating these transitions and help pupils in the early years to develop a positive approach to new experiences and to become confident to try new activities. They also help to prepare pupils for changes that may occur in their routines. While these areas are identified in the Foundation Stage curriculum (DfEE/QCA 2000a), they may remain important goals for some pupils throughout their education; schedules can be helpful in promoting these aspects of the curriculum at all ages and for all ability levels.

The National Curriculum identifies communication and working with others as key skills necessary across the curriculum (DfEE/QCA 1999a, b). QCA (2001b) guidance for teaching pupils with learning difficulties also identifies the need to develop early thinking skills. Critical areas may include recognising and obtaining information, predicting and anticipating, understanding cause and effect and linking objects, events and experiences. Structured Teaching's ways of using visual schedules help to address these areas. In particular, visual schedules help with social goals of working with others, listening and responding. For example, schedules enable pupils to understand who the teacher is for a particular lesson, which facilitates attending to that person and participating in their lesson. Social situations can be anticipated by pupils with autism and these appropriate expectations help their overall functioning in social and interpersonal situations.

The National Curriculum also includes improving own learning and performance as a key skill (DfEE/QCA 1999a, b). Making choices and communicating preferences are crucial precursors for developing these skills. Many pupils with ASD have difficulties with the simplest of choices. Once secure in the use of a schedule, choices are more easily incorporated into their routine in order to understand and develop this choice-making skill.

Visual schedules, by allowing pupils with ASD to function more independently in their environments, also facilitate access to aspects of PSHE and citizenship and are helpful in teaching pupils to manage and moderate their behaviour.

In summary, daily schedules can help in many important curriculum areas. They can facilitate the Early Learning Goals of personal, social and emotional development by promoting positive dispositions to learn, self-confidence and motivation. They also help to establish routines and prepare for change. Visual schedules help to promote key skills including communication, working with others and problem solving. These may include aspects such as recognising and obtaining information; predicting and anticipating; understanding cause and effect; linking objects, events and experiences, as suggested in the curriculum guidance for teaching pupils with learning difficulties (QCA 2001b). Visual schedules also promote early thinking skills, such as learning to remember. Daily living skills, community skills, personal and social skills, and managing one's own behaviour are also promoted by the use of schedules. Finally, schedules can be helpful in PSHE and citizenship, promoting participation, making real choices and decisions, and meeting and working with others. Schedules can also facilitate work-related learning.

The third area of Structured Teaching, described in Chapter 6, is work systems. These are the systematic, individualised and meaningful strategies that are developed to help pupils with ASD complete specific tasks. Individualised work systems help keep pupils organised so that they can function independently and effectively in a variety of different activities. These systematic strategies can also be very effective in increasing access to different aspects of the curriculum.

Work systems are especially helpful in organising pupils with ASD as they work on specific tasks in specific areas. For example, independent work systems are crucial for promoting aspects of the Early Learning Goal, personal, social and emotional development. These include independence in carrying out activities, attention, concentration and sitting quietly, independence within the environment, and independent use of resources. Children in the early years should increase their confidence, try new activities, and attend, concentrate and sit quietly when appropriate. Work systems help young pupils to work towards these goals and can be adapted for older pupils who may need to continue to work towards these areas of learning as a priority.

Curriculum guidance for pupils with learning difficulties (QCA 2001b) highlights the need to develop organisation and study skills, which are much more easily achieved through individual work systems. The work system is also an excellent strategy to help pupils to fully participate in curricular activities by focusing on the learning environment, organisation and sequencing, motivation and concentration, and communication.

This curriculum guidance also identifies the need for pupils to develop personal autonomy, to make meaningful choices and to communicate their choices, in all subjects, and during all key stages. Examples include increasing attention, interest, motivation, managing work time independently, completing tasks and taking responsibility for tasks by working independently. Guidance for PSHE and citizenship (QCA 2001f) describes the need to develop personal autonomy, managing behaviour and developing control across the curriculum. Access to the curriculum will be enhanced if pupils are encouraged to develop these skills. These are major reasons why independent work systems were developed by Division TEACCH and these systems provide an excellent foundation for promoting these skills.

Although independent work systems are initially practised in independent work areas, they can also be used to encourage pupils with ASD to interact with their classmates, thus encouraging pupils to develop the key skill of working with others, which is required in all curriculum areas.

Guidance for PSHE and citizenship indicates key learning areas, including taking responsibility, feeling positive, developing personal autonomy, and making choices. By promoting independent functioning and clarifying the concept of 'finished' so that pupils feel a real sense of accomplishment, the work system can be instrumental in achieving these goals. The work system also facilitates generalisation by providing systematic strategies that pupils can use in many different settings. This is an important goal in, for example, PSHE and citizenship, which encourages breadth of opportunities. Work system strategies can also be effective for work-related learning at older ages. Pupils in secondary schools can be involved in work-related learning, which requires independent functioning, through the use of their work systems.

Work systems can also help pupils to achieve the objective of being included in mainstream classrooms. Many pupils with ASD can be successful in mainstream settings if they have these systematic, organised and visual strategies. By helping pupils to overcome difficulties with organisation, teachers may be able to reduce some of the barriers to learning that pupils with ASD may face.

In summary, the work system promotes the Early Learning Goal personal, social and emotional development, including independence in carrying out activities, independence in the environment, independent use of resources, concentration and sitting quietly. Key National Curriculum skills include communication and working with others; both can be facilitated through the use of work systems. Guidance for planning, teaching and assessing the curriculum for pupils with learning difficulties includes organisation and study skills; work systems are excellent strategies for developing these skills. Personal, social and health education, and citizenship, including managing one's own behaviour, self-control, personal autonomy, making choices, taking responsibility, and feeling positive, can all be facilitated through the work system. Finally, another aspect of the school curriculum that the work system can promote is work-related learning.

Chapter 7 reviews visual structure and information and its value in accessing the National Curriculum. Visual structure can be used to differentiate tasks for pupils with ASD helping to organise, clarify and highlight important and relevant information. It can be extremely helpful for instructing pupils about how to complete specific tasks and how to use required materials.

The principles of inclusion identified in the National Curriculum (DfEE/QCA 1999a, b), identify the need to set suitable learning challenges, overcome potential barriers to learning and respond to individual learning needs. Structured Teaching, and especially its use of visual structure, adapts visual materials, activities and tasks to the appropriate developmental level for each individual pupil.

Adaptations, clarification and organisation of materials are especially helpful for pupils in the Foundation Stage. Examples illustrate how visually structured activities can help pupils develop basic skills within the Foundation Stage curriculum, for example mathematical development or hand–eye coordination. Similar clarification and organisation are helpful to pupils with ASD and additional learning difficulties.

Visual structure can also help pupils to achieve in specific subject lessons. For example, visual organisation, clarity and instructions may enable pupils to engage in experimentation and investigation in science, using a range of equipment in familiar and relevant situations. In mathematics and numeracy lessons, visual cues can highlight relevant information to keep pupils focused and engaged and may, for example, remind pupils which operations they need to use. Structured activities also help with literacy, for example writing about events and personal experiences linked to a variety of familiar incidents from stories using a prepared visual template. Visual instructions can be incorporated into PE lessons, for example in activities requiring pupils to perform basic skills in travelling, and choosing and linking skills and actions in short movement phases. In design and technology, visual cues enable pupils to assemble, join and combine materials or to plan, make and reflect.

Visual cues can encourage pupils to solve simple problems and develop early thinking skills, and provide pupils with opportunities to be involved with visual and/or tactile recording that reflect their widening range of experiences.

Visual information is also helpful outside the classroom. For example, it can promote the work of pupils in developing their entrepreneurial skills in Key Stage 3, to prepare pupils for broadening their experiences and in work-related learning.

Visual symbols can also be helpful in monitoring behaviours in a wide range of contexts. For example, highlighting important information can also be helpful in achieving targets in PSHE relating to personal hygiene.

Clearly these visual strategies can help pupils to access a very wide range of curriculum areas. The principle underpinning these approaches emphasises the importance of individualised assessment. In order to develop the most effective levels of structure for a pupil, it is essential that careful assessment of the individual needs of the pupil be carried out. This will include an assessment of the pupil's level of visual cognition and what degree of structure ensures greatest understanding and independence. The four elements of Structured Teaching then combine to provide the pupil with the level of structure that helps him to understand and to access the curriculum. Different pupils will have different requirements, hence the examples in this book serve only to illustrate how the approach can be used. The challenge now is to assess individual needs and to develop structured approaches that facilitate teaching and learning for each individual.

It is also crucial to regularly monitor and assess the levels of structure a pupil is using. A pupil's needs will change over time and different levels of structure may be required for some pupils in different contexts. For example, a pupil may need greater structure in an unfamiliar classroom with unfamiliar peers, or when he enters a new context such as work experience. While some pupils may need constant levels of structure for a long period, others may have fairly rapidly changing requirements. This can only be provided through careful monitoring of the structure. Appendix B provides a pro forma for recording a pupil's level of structure. This can be used to record the levels of structure a pupil requires and to achieve consistency of approach.

Finally, independent tasks also need to be monitored carefully. While some pupils will benefit from some repetition, others may become bored if they are required to repeat tasks too often. Progress needs to be assessed and monitored to record pupil progression. In addition, independent tasks should be linked to areas of learning and referenced to specific aspects of the curriculum. For example, a pupil may have a series of tasks for independent work during the literacy hour. Tasks may relate to the literacy lesson and are cross-referenced to the literacy strategy, or linked to a pupil's IEP targets. Either way, the pupil's progress needs to be monitored and recorded. Appendix C provides a pro forma for recording achievement and progress for independent tasks.

The short summary and review in this chapter only touches the surface. There are undoubtedly numerous other ways that the Structured Teaching approach can support, enhance and facilitate implementation of the curriculum. A real strength of Structured Teaching is its ability to combine with a number of other approaches, philosophies, or curricula to enhance the development of pupils with ASD. Structured Teaching provides a framework for delivering the curriculum for pupils with specific learning styles. Within this framework, the content of the curriculum can be, and should be, broad and balanced. If the framework of Structured Teaching is used to deliver the curriculum, opportunities can then be provided for pupils with ASD to access a curriculum that is appropriate for their needs, including varied approaches such as music interaction therapy, physical exercise and social skills programmes as well as the National Curriculum.

Structured Teaching is an 'autism friendly' way of organising and presenting information to people with ASD. Deriving its strategies from the growing literature on the neurological basis of autism, Structured Teaching offers countless strategies, approaches and techniques that those implementing the National Curriculum, or any other relevant resource for pupils with ASD, will find extremely helpful. The examples offered in this book are just a starting point of what can be accomplished. Hopefully, these examples will inspire teachers, parents and other interested professionals, who are starting with the exciting task of providing pupils with ASD access to the many rich and important opportunities that the whole curriculum, including the National Curriculum, provides.

Appendix A: Organisation of the curriculum

The curriculum consists of a number of elements to which all pupils are entitled. The Early Learning Goals and National Curriculum subjects should provide opportunities for spiritual, moral, social and cultural development and should promote key skills and thinking skills across the curriculum. The curriculum is organised into the Foundation Stage, covering the Early Learning Goals, and four key stages. Core and non-core foundation subjects are identified for all key stages, together with other requirements (DfEE/QCA 1999a, b). Table A summarises the organisation of the curriculum including early years, primary and secondary provision.

Programmes of study identify what pupils should be taught in each subject during each key stage and are used for planning. In addition, the National Literacy Strategy (NLS) provides a framework with detailed objectives for planning and teaching National Curriculum English: 'reading' and 'writing' at Key Stages 1 to 3 (DfEE 1998, 2001). The National Numeracy Strategy (NNS) provides a similarly detailed framework for planning and teaching National Curriculum mathematics in Key Stages 1 and 2 (DfEE 1999).

Attainment targets are identified for each subject to reflect pupil attainment at the end of each key stage. Level descriptions describe the range of performance for each attainment target. For example, Science at Key Stage 1 comprises four attainment targets (scientific enquiry, life processes and living things, materials and their properties, physical processes); six level descriptions indicate pupil performance during the key stage for each attainment target.

In addition, QCA curriculum guidance for 'planning, teaching and assessing the curriculum for pupils with learning difficulties' provides support for schools in developing and planning the curriculum, developing skills and subject planning, teaching and assessing. Performance descriptions allow teachers to assess pupils' attainment up to level 1 of the National Curriculum (P levels 1–8) (QCA 2001a).

Table A: Organisation of the curriculum.

Foundation Stage Ages 3–5 Preschool Nursery Reception	Early Learning Goals	• Personal, social and emotional development • Communication, language and literacy • Mathematical development • Knowledge and understanding of the world • Physical development • Creative development
National Curriculum Primary Key Stage 1: ages 5–7 (Years 1 and 2) Key Stage 2: ages 7–11 (Years 3–6) **Secondary** Key Stage 3: ages 11–14 (Years 7–9) Key Stage 4: ages 14–16 (Years 10 and 11)	General requirements of the National Curriculum	• Including the statement on and principles for inclusion
	Key skills (embedded in the National Curriculum)	• Communication • Application of number • Information technology • Working with others • Improving own learning and performance • Problem solving
	Thinking skills (embedded in the National Curriculum)	• Information-processing skills • Reasoning skills • Enquiry skills • Creative thinking skills • Evaluation skills
	Core subjects	• English (and NLS) • Mathematics (and NNS) • Science
	Non-core foundation subjects	• Information and communication technology • Design and technology • History • Geography • Art and design • Music • Physical education • Modern foreign languages (Key Stages 3 and 4)
	Other requirements	• Personal, social and health education and citizenship • Religious education • Sex education • Preparation for adult life, including accredited courses and work-related learning • Financial capability • Enterprise education • Education for sustainable development

Appendix B: Summary of structure

Name: _____ **Date:**

_____

Motivators (to be used for 'first, then' routine or for choice)	
Physical structure (designated areas, reduction of distractions)	
Schedule (length, level of visual information, transition area, how it is checked)	

Work system (left to right, sequencing, written)	
Visual structure (strategies for differentiation: clarity, organisation, instructions)	
Opportunities for communication within the structure (communication system)	

Appendix C: Recording sheet for monitoring independent tasks

Name: _____ Curriculum area: _____

Independent task	Curriculum reference or IEP target	Assessment (including level of prompting required)	Date and initials

Bibliography

American Psychiatric Association (1994) *Diagnostic and Statistical Manual of Mental Disorders*, 4th edn (*DSM-IV*). Washington DC: American Psychiatric Association.

Asperger, H. (1944) 'Die "autistischen psychopathen" im Kindesalter', *Archiv fur Psychiatrie Nervenkrankheiten*, **117**, 76–136. Translated by Frith, U. (ed.) (1999) *Autism and Asperger Syndrome*, 37–9. Cambridge: University Press.

Association of Head Teachers of Autistic Children and Adults (AHTACA) (1986) *The Special Curricular Needs of Autistic Children*. London: AHTACA.

Berger, A. and Gross, J. (1999) *Teaching the Literacy Hour in an Inclusive Classroom*. London: David Fulton.

Bishop, D. M. (2000) 'What's so special about Asperger syndrome? The need for further exploration of the borderlands of autism', in Klin, A., Volkmar, F. R. and Sparrow, S. S. (eds) *Asperger Syndrome*, 254–77. New York: Guilford Press.

Bondy, A. S. and Frost, L. A. (1994) 'The picture exchange system', *Focus on Autistic Behaviour* **9**(3), 1–19.

Byers, R. (1998) 'Personal and social development for pupils with learning difficulties', in Tilstone, C., Florian, L. and Rose, R. (eds) *Promoting Inclusive Practice*, 39–61. London: Routledge.

Cumine, V., Leach, J. and Stevenson, G. (1998) *Asperger Syndrome: A practical guide for teachers*. London: David Fulton.

Cumine, V., Leach, J. and Stevenson, G. (2000) *Autism in the Early Years*. London: David Fulton.

Davidson, G. (1996) 'Using OFSTED criteria to develop classroom practice', *Teaching Geography*, January, 11–14.

Department for Education (DfE) (1995) *The National Curriculum*. London: HMSO.

Department for Education and Employment (DfEE) (1998) *The National Literacy Strategy: Framework for teaching*. London: DfEE.

DfEE (1999) *The National Numeracy Strategy*. London: DfEE.

DfEE (2000) *The National Literacy Strategy: Supporting pupils with special educational needs in the literacy hour*. London: DfEE.

DfEE (2001) *Key Stage 3 National Strategy: Framework for teaching English: Years 7, 8 and 9*. London: DfEE.

Department for Education and Employment (DfEE)/Qualifications and Curriculum Authority (QCA) (1999a) *The National Curriculum: Handbook for primary teachers in England*. London: DfEE/QCA.

DfEE/QCA (1999b) *The National Curriculum: Handbook for secondary teachers in England*. London: DfEE/QCA.

DfEE/QCA (2000a) *Curriculum Guidance for the Foundation Stage*. London: QCA.

DfEE/QCA (2000b) *Religious Education: A scheme of work for Key Stages 1 and 2*. London: DfEE/QCA.

Department for Education and Skills (DfES) (2001a) *Inclusive Schooling: Children with special educational needs*. London: DfES

DfES (2001b) *Special Educational Needs: Code of practice*. London: DfES.

DfES (2001c) *The National Numeracy Strategy: The daily mathematics lesson: Guidance to support pupils with Autistic Spectrum Disorders*. London: DfES.

DfES (2002) *ASD – Guidance from the autism working group*. London: DfES.

Frith, U. (1989) *Autism: Explaining the enigma*. Oxford: Blackwell.

Gagnon, L., Mottron, L. and Jonette, Y. (1997) 'Questioning the validity of the Semantic–Pragmatic Syndrome diagnosis', *Autism* **1**, 37–55.

Grandin, T. (1995) *Thinking in Pictures and Other Reports from my Life with Autism*. New York: Doubleday.

Gray, C. (1998) 'Social stories and comic strip conversations with students with Asperger Syndrome and High Functioning Autism', in Schopler, E., Mesibov, G. and Kunce, L. (eds) *Asperger Syndrome or High Functioning Autism?*, 167–98. New York: Plenum Press.

Hodgdon, L. (1995) *Visual Strategies for Improving Communication*. Michigan: QuirkRoberts.

Jordan, R. (1999) *Autistic Spectrum Disorders: An introductory handbook for practitioners*. London: David Fulton.

Jordan, R. and Powell, S. (1990a) *The Special Curricular Needs of Autistic Children: Learning and thinking skills*. London: AHTACA.

Jordan, R. and Powell, S. (1990b) 'Autism and the National Curriculum', *British Journal of Special Education* **17**, 140–2.

Jordan, R. and Powell, S. (1995) *Understanding and Teaching Children with Autism*. Chichester: Wiley.

Jordan, R., Jones, G. and Murray, D. (1998) *Educational Interventions for Children with Autism: A literature review of recent and current research*. Sudbury: DfEE.

Kanner, L. (1943) 'Autistic disturbances of affective contact', *Nervous Child* **2**, 217–50.

Mesibov, G. B. and Shea, V. (undated) 'The culture of autism: from theoretical understanding to educational practice'. Available at http://www/autismuk.com [accessed September 2002].

Mesibov, G. B., Adams, L. W. and Klinger, L. G. (1997) *Autism: Understanding the disorder*. New York: Plenum Press.

National Curriculum Council (NCC) (1989) *A Curriculum for All*. York: NCC.

Norwich, B. (1996) 'Special needs education for all: Connective specialisation and ideological impurity', *British Journal of Special Education* **23**(3), 100–3.

Ozonoff, S. (1995) 'Executive function impairments in autism', in Schopler, E. and Mesibov, G. (eds) *Learning and Cognition in Autism*, 199–220. New York: Plenum.

Ozonoff, S., Pennington, B. and Rogers, S. (1991) 'Executive function deficits in high-functioning autistic individuals: Relationship to theory of mind', *Journal of Child Psychology and Psychiatry* **32**, 1107–22.

Powell, S. (ed.) (2000) *Helping Children with Autism to Learn*. London: David Fulton.

Prior, M. and Hoffman, W. (1990) 'Neuropsychological testing of autistic children through an exploration with frontal lobe tasks', *Journal of Autism and Developmental Disorders* **20**, 130–9.

Qualifications and Curriculum Authority (QCA) (2000) *Citizenship at Key Stages 3 and 4*. London: QCA.

QCA (2001a) *Planning, Teaching and Assessing the Curriculum for Pupils with Learning Difficulties: General guidelines*. London: QCA.

QCA (2001b) *Planning, Teaching and Assessing the Curriculum for Pupils with Learning Difficulties: Developing skills*. London: QCA.

QCA (2001c) *Planning, Teaching and Assessing the Curriculum for Pupils with Learning Difficulties: English*. London: QCA.

QCA (2001d) *Planning, Teaching and Assessing the Curriculum for Pupils with Learning Difficulties: Mathematics*. London: QCA.

QCA (2001e) *Planning, Teaching and Assessing the Curriculum for Pupils with Learning Difficulties: Science*. London: QCA.

QCA (2001f) *Planning, Teaching and Assessing the Curriculum for Pupils with Learning Difficulties: Personal, social and health education and citizenship*. London: QCA.

QCA (2001g) *Planning, Teaching and Assessing the Curriculum for Pupils with Learning Difficulties: Religious education*. London: QCA.

QCA (2001h) *Planning, Teaching and Assessing the Curriculum for Pupils with Learning Difficulties: History*. London: QCA.

QCA/DfEE (2000) *Science: A scheme of work for Key Stage 3*. London: QCA.

Quill, K. (ed.) (1995) *Teaching Children with Autism: Strategies to enhance communication and socialisation*. New York: Delmar.

Rose, R. (1991) 'A jigsaw approach to group work', *British Journal of Special Education* **18**(2), 31–3.

Rose, R. (1998) 'The curriculum: a vehicle for inclusion or a lever for exclusion?', in Tilstone, C., Florian, L. and Rose, R. (eds) *Promoting Inclusive Practice*, 27–38. London: Routledge.

Rose, R. and Howley, M. (2001) 'Entitlement or denial? The curriculum and its influences upon inclusion processes', in O'Brien, T. (ed.) *Enabling Inclusion: Blue skies . . . dark clouds?*, 65–80. London: The Stationery Office.

Sainsbury, C. (2000) *Martian in the Playground*. Bristol: Lucky Duck.

Schopler, E. and Mesibov, G. (1995) *Learning and Cognition in Autism*. New York: Plenum

Schopler, E., Mesibov, G. and Hearsey, K. (1995) 'Structured teaching in the TEACCH system', in Schopler, E. and Mesibov, G. (eds) *Learning and Cognition in Autism*, 243–68. New York: Plenum.

Szatmari, P. (1998) 'Differential diagnosis of Asperger disorder', in Schopler, E., Mesibov, G. B. and Kunce, L. J. (eds) *Asperger Syndrome or High-functioning Autism?*, 61–76. New York: Plenum Press.

Watson, L., Lord, C., Schaffer, B. and Schopler, E. (1989) *Teaching Spontaneous Communication to Autistic and Developmentally Handicapped Children*. New York: Irvington.

Wing, L. (1981) 'Asperger's syndrome: A clinical account', *Psychological Medicine* **11**, 115–30.

Wing, L. (1996) *The Autistic Spectrum: A guide for parents and professionals*. London: Constable.

Wing, L. and Gould, J. (1979) 'Severe impairments of social interaction and associated abnormalities in children: epidemiology and classification', *Journal of Autism and Childhood Schizophrenia* **9**, 11–29.

Wolff, S. (1998) 'Schizoid personality in childhood: The links with Asperger syndrome, schizophrenia spectrum disorders and elective mutism', in Schopler, E., Mesibov, G. B. and Kunce, L. J. (eds) *Asperger Syndrome or High-functioning Autism?*, 123–42. New York: Plenum Press.

World Health Organisation (WHO) (1992) *The ICD-10 Classification of Mental and Behavioural Disorders. Diagnostic criteria for research*. Geneva: WHO.

Index

Printed in the United States
81706LV00001B